Table of Contents

The Flame Imperishable

Catholicism in the Halls of Middle-earth's History

by

Dr. ant

Copyright 2024 Dr. ant. All rights reserved.

No part of this book may be reproduced in any form or by any electronic or mechanical means including information storage and retrieval systems, without permission in writing from the author. The only exception is by a reviewer, who may quote short excerpts in a review.

Although the author and publisher have made every effort to ensure that the information in this book was correct at press time, the author and publisher do not assume and hereby disclaim any liability to any party for any loss, damage, or disruption caused by errors or omissions, whether such errors or omissions result from negligence, accident, or any other cause.

This publication is designed to provide accurate and authoritative information with regard to the subject matter covered. It is sold with the understanding that the publisher is not engaged in rendering professional services. If legal advice or other expert assistance is required, the services of a competent professional should be sought.

The fact that an organization or website is referred to in this work as a citation and/or a potential source of further information does not mean that the author or the publisher endorses the information the organization or website may provide or recommendations it may make.

Please remember that Internet websites listed in this work may have changed or disappeared between when this work was written and when it is read.

Contents

Introduction

In the realm of literature and theology, few works have stirred as much intrigue and scholarly debate as the mythopoeic universe crafted by J.R.R. Tolkien. At the heart of Tolkien's profound narrative lies a tapestry of themes resonant with Roman Catholic doctrine, interwoven with the threads of creation, providence, and eschatology, painted against the sprawling backdrop of Middle-earth. This oeuvre seeks to explore and defend the Catholic doctrines as mirrored in Tolkien's legendarium, promising a journey through the vistas of a world where the light of faith battles the shadows of despair, where the concepts of divine benevolence, omnipotence, omniscience, and omnipresence are not mere abstracts but lived realities.

The discourse on the creation, initiated in "The Silmarillion," speaks volumes of the Catholic notion of a universe brought into being by a singular, supreme act of will – that of Eru Ilúvatar. This opens a profound dialogue with the theological perspectives on free will and the problem of evil, as seen in the discord sown by Melkor. These narratives, while mythic in scope, engage with such cardinal doctrines of creation ex nihilo and the introduction of sin into a primordially good creation.

Focusing on providence, Tolkien's tales are teeming with instances where divine foresight and intervention are palpable, guiding the affairs of Middle-earth towards a predestined end – often manifesting through the concept of eucatastrophe, a sudden turn of events for the better that signifies the indomitable will of the divine. Herein lies a complex tapestry of belief and reality, where characters navigate the tension between free will and destiny, a thematic exploration that resonates deeply with the Catholic understanding of divine providence.

The eschatological themes woven into the fabric of Tolkien's narratives invite reflection on the Catholic vision of the end times. Tolkien's portrayal of history moving towards a definitive consummation, paralleled with motifs of resurrection and the final defeat of evil, mirrors the Christian hope in the Second Coming and the new creation. Through characters and events, Tolkien nuances the concept of an eschatological kingdom characterized by peace and justice, reflecting the ultimate realization of God's providential plan.

The methodology employed in this exploration adopts a multidisciplinary approach, drawing from theology, philosophy, and literary analysis to dissect and interpret the Catholic elements in Tolkien's works. This analysis endeavors to illuminate the intricate ways in which Tolkien's Catholicism informs and shapes his mythology, arguing that Tolkien's fictional universe serves not only as a monumental achievement in world-building but also as a profound theological allegory.

This work is divided into thematic chapters that sequentially address the central motifs of creation, providence, and eschatology within Tolkien's universe, enriched by a detailed examination of parallel Catholic doctrines. Through this structure, the reader is invited to delve deeper into the theological underpinnings of Middle-earth and explore the multifaceted ways in which these doctrines manifest in the narrative.

At its core, this book aims to bridge the worlds of literary scholarship and theological inquiry, offering a comprehensive analysis that satisfies both the academic and the spiritual seeker. It endeavors to provide an academically rigorous, yet accessible narrative that elucidates the Catholic dimensions of Tolkien's work, opening new avenues for understanding and interpreting his mythic creation. It is a call to those who wish to explore the depths of Tolkien's imagination, guided by the lights of faith, reason, and scholarship.

As we embark on this journey through Middle-earth, let us be mindful of the profound truths that lie hidden within its stories. What at first glance appears to be a mere fantasy narrative unfolds into a rich theological tapestry, reflecting the eternal dance between light and darkness, free will and divine providence, death and rebirth. Here, we find not only entertainment but also enlightenment, not just stories but a reflection of our deepest beliefs and hopes.

This introduction, therefore, sets the stage for a scholarly pilgrimage, a quest into the heart of Middle-earth to uncover the luminous strands of Catholic doctrine interlaced within its stories. It is an invitation to discover how Tolkien's work can enrich our understanding of creation, illuminate our grasp of providence, and inspire our hopes in the eschatological promise of a renewed creation.

In undertaking this scholarly endeavor, we align ourselves with a tradition of thought that sees in literature not merely the creative expression of the human mind but a medium through which the divine communicates truths about Himself, the world, and our place within it. Through the analytical lens of this work, we appreciate Tolkien not just as a master storyteller but as a subtle theologian, whose myths carry within them echoes of eternal truths.

As the following chapters will demonstrate, Tolkien's mythology, while rooted in his time, personal experiences, and scholarly pursuits, transcends these to speak to universal truths about the human condition, the struggle between good and evil, and the ultimate hope of redemption. By the end of this exploration, it is the sincere hope that the reader will not only garner a deeper appreciation for Tolkien's artistry and insight but also a richer understanding of the Catholic faith as it dialogues with contemporary culture through the medium of myth.

Let us, therefore, begin our journey with open hearts and minds, ready to explore the vast landscapes of Middle-earth, guided by the light of faith, reason, and imagination. In doing so, we may discover not just the depth and richness of Tolkien's creative vision but the timeless truths and beauty of the Catholic faith it reflects.

The Light of Eä: An Overview of Tolkien's Mythopoeic Universe

The world of J.R.R. Tolkien, a canvas of unimaginable depth, is a realm where the forces of good and evil continually clash, where heroes are forged in the fires of adversity, and where the faintest light of hope can dispel the darkest shadows. At the heart of this universe, known as Eä, lies an intricate tapestry of myth, legend, and profound theological inquiry. To explore Tolkien's creation is to embark on a journey through a world that, while fictional, offers profound insights into our understanding of creation, providence, and eschatology.

The beginning of all things in Tolkien's universe is marked by a singular, harmonious vision, encapsulated in the Music of the Ainur, led by Eru Ilúvatar, the One. This music, a divine symphony of free will and predestination, weaves the fabric of reality, setting the stage for the unfolding drama of Middle-Earth and its inhabitants. Through this act of creation, Ilúvatar introduces the central themes of harmony, discord, and the eventual resolution of good over evil, themes that reflect the Catholic understanding of a universe guided by a benevolent, omnipotent creator.

Within the mythopoeic tapestry of Eä, the Ainur, divine beings who partake in the creation of the world through their music, play a pivotal role. Their melodies are not merely artistic expressions but acts of creation in themselves, shaping the physical and moral order of the world. This portrayal of sub-creation under the guidance of a supreme deity mirrors the Catholic doctrine of creation, where all that exists does so through the will and word of God. Tolkien's cosmogony, thus, becomes a metaphor for the divine act of creation, reflecting the beauty, complexity, and purpose inherent in the Catholic worldview.

The entry of Melkor, the Ainur who introduces discord into the Music, marks the inception of evil into Tolkien's world. His rebellion, stemming from pride and the desire for dominion, illustrates the Catholic understanding of evil as a privation of good and a corruption of free will. Melkor's actions set forth the narrative of sin, fall, and the hope for redemption, a storyline that resonates deeply with the Catholic tradition of salvation history.

The Valar, divine custodians of the world, further highlight the Catholic themes of guardianship, stewardship, and divine will. Their governance and care for Eä reflect the Catholic principle of Providence, the belief in God's active involvement in His creation to guide it towards its ultimate good. Through the Valar, Tolkien presents a universe imbued with purpose and direction, counteracting the notion of a mechanistic world devoid of divine presence.

The creation of Elves and Men introduces into Tolkien's universe beings endowed with free will, capable of choosing between good and evil. This delineation between the immortal Elves and mortal Men encapsulates the Catholic teachings on the nature of the human soul, its eternal destiny, and the profound mystery of death. Tolkien's depiction of Elves and Men, their destinies intertwined yet distinct, serves as a narrative exploration of Catholic anthropology, eschatology, and the paradox of free will in a divinely ordained cosmos.

Tolkien's mythopoeic universe, with its intricate layers and profound themes, serves not merely as a backdrop for epic tales of heroism and adventure but as a fertile ground for theological and philosophical inquiry. The struggle against evil, the journey towards redemption, and the ultimate triumph of good reflect the Catholic vision of human history as a conflict between sin and grace, guided by divine providence towards its eschatological fulfillment.

The role of prophecy, divine revelation, and the intercession of higher powers within Tolkien's works further enriches the theological dimensions of his universe. The foreseeing of future events, the guidance provided by characters such as Gandalf, and the intervention of Ilúvatar at critical moments underscore a reality governed by a divine plan, accessible through faith, hope, and the discernment of divine will.

The sacramental imagination of Tolkien's world—where material elements carry an inner spiritual significance—echoes the Catholic sacramental understanding of reality. Through elements such as lembas bread and the waters of the Silmaril, Tolkien weaves a sense of the sacred into the fabric of his fictional universe, inviting reflection on the presence of the divine in the everyday.

The Marian figure of Galadriel, with her purity, wisdom, and intercessory power, embodies Catholic teachings on the role of the Virgin Mary as the mediatrix of grace. Through Galadriel, as well as other female figures in Middle-Earth, Tolkien presents models of virtue, courage, and humility, aligning with the Catholic veneration of Mary and the saints.

In the face of evil and suffering, the residents of Middle-Earth exhibit a profound sense of hope, a central tenet of Catholic eschatology. This hope is not a naive optimism but a steadfast belief in the ultimate victory of good over evil, of light over darkness. Characters such as Samwise Gamgee, with their unwavering faith in the possibility of redemption and renewal, serve as embodiments of this theological virtue, inspiring readers to perceive the gleams of grace even in the darkest moments.

The narrative of death and the afterlife, particularly in the tales of Men and Elves, offers a reflective lens on Catholic beliefs regarding the soul, judgment, and the promise of eternal life. Tolkien's exploration of these themes challenges the modern denial of death's reality and the reduction of human existence to the material plane, proposing instead a vision of life as a journey towards a transcendent horizon.

Finally, the beauty of creation, as depicted in the landscapes of Middle-Earth, from the rolling hills of the Shire to the ethereal realms of Valinor, calls to mind the Catholic sacramentality of the natural world. In Tolkien's universe, creation reveals the glory of its Creator, inviting contemplation and stewardship, and standing as a testament to the divine splendor that pervades the world.

In conclusion, Tolkien's mythopoeic universe, with its rich tapestry of themes—ranging from the drama of creation to the hope of redemption—offers a profound medium for exploring and defending Catholic doctrine. The Light of Eä, as it shines forth from the pages of Tolkien's works, illuminates the truths of Catholic faith, inviting readers to perceive in his fiction echoes of the eternal, the transcendent, and the divine.

References:

Genesis Through Elven Eyes: The Silmarillion and Catholic Creation

In the intricate tapestry of Tolkien's mythopoetic universe, *The Silmarillion* stands as a testament to the creation and shaping of a world rich in lore, beauty, and complexity. From the very outset, this narrative invites us into an exploration of creation that resonates deeply with Catholic thought, weaving a tale that echoes the genesis of our own world while unveiling the divine fingerprints left upon Middle-earth. It is through Elven eyes that we are afforded a glimpse into this genesis, revealing a narrative that, while distinct, harmonizes with the Catholic understanding of creation, providence, and eschatology.

The beginning of all things, as told in *The Silmarillion*, unfolds with Eru Ilúvatar, who brings the universe into being through His word, paralleling the Christian doctrine where God speaks the universe into existence. This act of creation through the Word finds a strong echo in the Gospel of John, binding the tales of Middle-earth to the core of Catholic creation narrative. The act of Ilúvatar does not merely breathe life into the cosmos but sets into motion a narrative of free will, divine providence, and eventual redemption, themes that find their counterparts in the Catholic understanding of the world's genesis.

Ilúvatar's introduction of the Ainur, and their subsequent role in shaping the world through the Music, unveils a parallel to the angelic hierarchy and their participation in God's creative act, as discussed in Catholic theology. In their music, we see an allegory for the order, harmony, and hierarchy of creation that Catholic doctrine espouses. The discord introduced by Melkor, mirroring the fall of Lucifer, introduces into Tolkien's universe the element of disharmony, which necessitates the intervention of a benevolent and omnipotent creator to restore balance and order, reminiscent of the Catholic understanding of original sin and redemption.

The central role of Elves in *The Silmarillion* allows a view of creation that encapsulates both the beauty and sorrow interwoven into the world by Ilúvatar's design. Their immortality, coupled with their deep connection to the fate of Arda, mirrors the Catholic belief in the eternal soul and its journey through history, marked by joy, suffering, and the hope of redemption. Elves, in their stewardship of Middle-earth, reflect the Catholic call to mankind to be caretakers of creation, echoing the responsibility entrusted to humanity to preserve and respect the integrity of the world.

Within the narrative, the creation of the Two Trees of Valinor stands as a significant theological symbol, resonating with the motifs of light and life found within Catholic tradition. The

Trees' illumination of Valinor before their downfall mirrors the light of Christ, which penetrates the darkness of sin to bring salvation to mankind. This imagery not only enriches the mythic landscape of Tolkien's universe but underscores a profound alignment with Catholic eschatological hope in the triumph of light over darkness.

The Silmarils, crafted by Fëanor, encapsulate the theme of divine light entrusted to the care of the created, bearing within them the hallowed light of the Two Trees. Their creation, theft, and the ensuing strife serve as a narrative exploration of the human condition, mirroring the Catholic contemplation on the use of free will, the allure of sin, and the arduous journey towards redemption. The quest for the Silmarils, laden with sacrifice, loss, and moments of grace, parallels the Christian pilgrimage towards salvation and the inherent tension between divine grace and human freedom.

The fall of Númenor, a tale of hubris, defiance, and divine judgment, echoes the Biblical narrative of the Tower of Babel. In their quest for immortality and power, the Númenóreans mirror humanity's perennial temptation to usurp the place of God, leading to their downfall. This story serves as a profound meditation on the Catholic understanding of pride as the root sin and the futility of attempting to attain divinity through human means. The cataclysm that engulfs Númenor is a stark reminder of the consequences of straying from the divine will, emphasizing the need for humility and submission to God's providential plan.

The role of providence in the unfolding drama of Middle-earth, as seen through the interplay of free will and divine guidance, underscores a core Catholic belief in a God who is both transcendent and intimately involved in the tapestry of history. The journey of characters such as Frodo and Aragorn illuminates the path of virtue, sacrifice, and reliance on providence, mirroring the spiritual journey that believers are called to embark upon. Their struggles, victories, and moments of despair reflect the pilgrimage of faith—a journey towards embracing the will of the Creator, acknowledging His omnipotence, and trusting in His ultimate plan for creation.

In conclusion, *The Silmarillion* through Elven eyes offers a mythic retelling of creation, fall, and redemption that deeply resonates with Catholic doctrine. It invites reflection on themes of divine providence, free will, and eschatological hope, providing a narrative space where the Catholic imagination can explore the mysteries of faith. Tolkien's creation, in its depth and beauty, not only enriches the literary landscape but serves as a bridge between myth and theology, inviting believers and seekers alike to ponder the divine mystery through the prism of Middle-earth's creation.

Elaborating Eru Ilúvatar: A Theological Perspective on Tolkien's Supreme Being

In the vast tapestry of Tolkien's mythopoeic legacy, the entity of Eru Ilúvatar stands as the foundational force of creation and the immanent sovereign of the universe. Fruitful discourse on Ilúvatar's character unfolds upon a theological plane where the intersection of Roman Catholic doctrine with Tolkien's creative vision illuminates the nature of the Supreme Being with a unique and compelling light.

Eru, the "One," called Ilúvatar, which denotes "Father of All," mirrors the singularity and paternal imagery central to the Christian conception of God. Ilúvatar is both distant from and close to his creation, embodying the dichotomy of transcendence and immanence that the Scholastic tradition has long pondered upon. This paradox is undeniably evident in the way Ilúvatar engages with His creation, simultaneously removed from the confines of the contingent world yet intimately involved in the unfolding of its history (Turner et al., 2020).

At the onset of the cosmos, Ilúvatar introduces the Ainur, divine beings conceived in the thought of the Creator, to participate in a symphony of creation. This Music of the Ainur resonates with the notion of logos, the divine word or reason, through which the world was spoken into being (John 1:1). Ilúvatar's supreme authority is manifest when, amid the discord introduced by Melkor, He weaves the cacophony into a greater harmony, asserting the omnipotence and omniscience that define Him (Carpenter, 2019).

The realm of Arda, wrought by the word of Ilúvatar and shaped by the hands of the Ainur, finds its destiny irrevocably bound to the will of the Creator. Ilúvatar's providence is a thread running through the history of Middle-earth, evident in the intrinsic goodness of the created order and the unfolding eucatastrophic moments that mark the epic tales (J.R.R. Tolkien, "Letters," No. 153).

In the fabric of Tolkien's work, Ilúvatar's Providence does not eliminate the reality of free will; rather, it affirms it. The Children of Ilúvatar, Elves, and Men are granted the agency to shape their path within the Creator's grand design, underscoring the Catholic belief in the harmonious coexistence of Divine Providence with human freedom (Catechism of the Catholic Church, 1993).

The eschatological promise of Ilúvatar is woven into the mythos as a reflection of hope, an assurance that the shadow and strife of the world are but a passage to a subsequent imbued reality where the Creator's purpose is fully realized. The thematic elements of death, immortality, and destiny in the lives of the

Children of Ilúvatar correspond with Catholic doctrine pertaining to the last things: death, judgment, heaven, and hell (Aquinas, Summa Theologica).

As Ilúvatar is the source of all that exists, so too is He the end toward which all creation moves. The overarching narrative of redemption and consummation finds its echo in Ilúvatar's plan for a world made right, a narrative arc deeply resonant with Catholic eschatological hope (Lewis, 1964).

The presence of Eru Ilúvatar throughout the myths also signifies an often overlooked aspect: His benevolence. In every act, from creation to the allowances made for the free actions of creatures, Ilúvatar's love is the driving force, much as the Catholic tradition upholds the love of God as central to the understanding of creation and divine action (1 John 4:8).

The enigmatic nature of Eru Ilúvatar also serves to embolden the faithful's awe before the majesty and mystery of God. Though glimpses of His thought are given in the tales and songs of the Eldar and the wisdom of the Istari, much remains beyond comprehension, echoing the Catholic sentiment of the apophatic tradition which acknowledges that God's essence is ultimately beyond human understanding (Pseudo-Dionysius, The Mystical Theology).

Eru's omnipresence is subtly demonstrated through the pervasive sense that the world itself is suffused with His awareness and care. This divine attribute reassures believers of God's ever-present gaze, overseeing with a providential eye the unfolding drama of human and elven histories, much like the Psalmist's conviction that one cannot flee from the presence of the Omniscient (Psalm 139:7-8).

In the unfolding epochs of Middle-earth, the presence of Eru Ilúvatar becomes a comforting certainty in moments of despair. Such assurance aligns with the Catholic understanding of the constancy of God's presence and aid, especially in times of turmoil and tribulation (Romans 8:28).

Ilúvatar's silence or perceived absence in certain epochs of Middle-earth's history summons the faithful to a deeper trust in the unknowable wisdom of the Creator. This mirrors the Catholic experience of the dark night of the soul, where the believer is called to faith even in the absence of felt divine presence (John of the Cross, The Dark Night).

The final act of history, referred to in the legendarium as the Dagor Dagorath, mirrors the Christian eschatological vision of a final confrontation between good and evil, wherein the reign of Ilúvatar will be absolute and unchallenged. It is a vision steeped in hope, the ultimate victory of light over darkness, and the renewal of all things in Ilúvatar (Revelation 21:1).

It is within the bounds of this theological framework that the role of Eru Ilúvatar in Tolkien's universe can be most fully appreciated. The Creator's characteristics and actions not only echo the core attributes ascribed to the God of Roman Catholicism but do so in a way that enhances the reader's appreciation of the divine mystery through the majesty of mythic narrative.

With this in mind, one can delve into the profound journey of discovery where Tolkien's fictional theology opens a vista into the timeless truths that have shaped and sustained the Catholic faith.

In the vast and intricate tapestry of J.R.R. Tolkien's mythopoeia, few elements are as transcendent and allegorical as the Music of the Ainur, a celestial symphony orchestrated by Eru Ilúvatar that gave birth to the physical universe and foretold the history of the world. **The Music of the Ainur: Harmony, Discord, and Free Will** serves not only as a majestic introduction to the creation of Eä but also encapsulates profound theological and philosophical themes that resonate with Roman Catholic doctrine.

The creation narrative within "The Silmarillion" where this concept is detailed is emblematic of a cosmic struggle between harmony and discord, reflecting the dual nature of creation and the existence of free will and its consequences. This narrative bears remarkable semblance to the Christian understanding of the world as a creation of God, marred by sin yet imbued with a divine purpose and destiny.

At the heart of this creation, myth is the figure of Eru Ilúvatar, a supreme deity whose omniscience, omnipotence, and omnipresence are manifested through the Ainur, his divine offspring. These Ainur, through their music, engage in a cosmic act of co-creation, each contributing their unique themes to the greater harmony orchestrated by Ilúvatar. This participatory act of creation mirrors the Catholic conception of the universe as a product of divine will and the cooperation of created beings with that will.

Melkor, the Ainur who introduces discord into the Music, represents the introduction of sin and evil into the world. His actions, stemming from pride and a desire to dominate rather than collaborate, echo the Fall of Lucifer and the presence of original sin in Christian theology. Like Lucifer, Melkor's discord disrupts the divine harmony but is ultimately incorporated into Ilúvatar's grand design, suggesting that even evil serves the purposes of the divine will, a concept that aligns with the Catholic understanding of providence.

Ilúvatar's acceptance and integration of Melkor's discord into the greater harmony imply a profound assertion of divine sovereignty and the ultimate triumph of good over evil. This theology reflects the Catholic belief in the omnipotence of God and the eventual realization of the divine plan despite human sinfulness and the presence of evil.

The Music of the Ainur also serves as a theological treatise on free will. The Ainur are granted the freedom to weave their own themes into the Music, reflecting the Catholic teaching that God endows His creatures with free will. This autonomy, however, does not negate the sovereignty of Ilúvatar but enriches the creation, imbuing it with genuine beauty and complexity.

However, with the gift of free will comes the potential for discord. Melkor's discordant music, born out of pride and rebellion, serves as a cautionary tale about the misuse of free will. It illustrates the Catholic teaching that while free will is a gift, it carries the responsibility of aligning one's will with that of the Creator. Misuse of free will leads to sin, which disrupts the harmony of creation.

This narrative simultaneously highlights the theme of redemption. Ilúvatar's ability to incorporate discord into a greater harmony without diminishing it speaks to the Catholic understanding of redemption. Despite the presence of evil, God's plan for the universe incorporates and transforms sin into a tool for greater good, a fundamental aspect of the Catholic concept of redemptive suffering.

The Music of the Ainur, thus, is not merely a myth of origin within Tolkien's universe but a profound allegory of the Catholic worldview. It encapsulates themes of creation, fall, free will, evil, providence, and redemption, presenting them in a narrative that is both epic and deeply theological.

Moreover, this narrative sets the stage for the moral and spiritual struggles that define Middle-Earth. The echoes of the Music's themes play out in the lives of Elves, Men, Dwarves, and Hobbits, illustrating that the cosmic drama of harmony and discord continues in the moral choices of individuals. This reinforces the Catholic teaching on the universal nature of the cosmic struggle between good and evil and the role of individual free will in that struggle.

Importantly, Tolkien's portrayal of this cosmic drama through the allegory of music speaks to the aesthetic dimension of Catholic theology. The beauty of the Music, even incorporating discord, underscores the Catholic belief in the transcendental quality of beauty as a reflection of the divine. It suggests that beauty, even in a fallen world, is a means through which the divine truth is revealed.

In conclusion, the Music of the Ainur serves as a foundational myth that not only sets the stage for the events of Tolkien's legendarium but also embodies profound theological and philosophical themes that resonate with Roman Catholic doctrine. It is a narrative of creation, fall, and redemption that reflects the complexity of the universe and the central role of free will within the divine plan. Through this myth, Tolkien offers a richly allegorical vision of reality that bridges the worlds of literature and theology, inviting reflection on the nature of God, creation, and the human condition.

References:

The Valor of Valinor: Understanding the Divine Council

The cosmology of Valinor, as elaborately depicted in Tolkien's legendarium, serves as a profound allegory of divine guidance, presence, and intervention, wonderfully mirroring the theological truths upheld by the Roman Catholic Church. In the unfolding narrative of Valinor, the divine council of the Valar, though not gods in the supreme sense, act as stewards of Eru Ilúvatar's creation, faithfully executing His will across the expanses of Middle-Earth. Their valor, decisions, and the subsequent interplay with both Maiar and mortal beings illuminate the Catholic understanding of a universe governed by divine providence and moral order.

At the forefront of this divine council stands Manwë, the King of the Valar, whose authority and benevolence reflect a governance guided by the principles of justice, love, and mercy. Through him, Tolkien encapsulates the ideal of divine kingship, an aspect deeply rooted in the Catholic tradition, showcasing a ruler whose leadership is an outpouring of service to the Other, rather than an assertion of power for its own sake. Manwë's rule, thus, becomes a lesson in the exercise of authority, vis-à-vis the fraternal and parental guidance extolled by the teachings of the Church.

Nienna, the patron of mercy and compassion, teaches the inhabitants of Middle-Earth the power of grief and pity. Her wisdom highlights the Roman Catholic understanding of suffering — not as a mere consequence of evil but as a path to deepened compassion and a means for divine grace to work profoundly within the world. Through her, Tolkien presents sorrow and grief as tools for spiritual refinement, echoing the Beatitudes' proclamation of the merciful and the mournful as blessed.

The greatest antagonist within Tolkien's mythology, Melkor, personifies the dangers of pride and the rejection of divine will. His fall from the highest of the Valar to Morgoth, the Dark Enemy, serves as a cautionary tale deeply reflective of Lucifer's fall in Christian theology. Melkor's choices, driven by pride and a desire for dominion over others, stand in stark opposition to the virtues exemplified by his fellow Valar, encapsulating the eternal struggle between good and evil, humility and arrogance — a central theme in Catholic doctrine.

In contrast, the narrative of the Valar showcases the virtue of free will exercised in harmony with Ilúvatar's vision. The Music of the Ainur, the creation myth at the heart of Tolkien's universe, highlights this beautifully. Each Ainur contributing to the symphony under Ilúvatar's direction symbolizes the Catholic understanding of free will: not as autonomy from the divine, but as cooperation with the Creator's grand design, where true freedom is found in submission to God's will.

The guardianship of the Valar over creation is another facet emblematic of Catholic teachings on stewardship and care for the created order. Yavanna's nurturing of the Two Trees of Valinor and her sorrow over their destruction reveals a profound respect for life and nature, an echo of the Catholic call to stewardship of the earth as God's creation.

The Valar's interventions in the affairs of Middle-Earth, albeit sparing and measured, underscore a providential governance that respects the autonomy and free will of its inhabitants. This mirrors the Catholic understanding of God's providence: never coercive, always respecting human freedom, yet intimately involved in the unfolding of the world's history toward its ultimate good.

The establishment of Valinor itself as a realm set apart, imbued with beauty and immortality, serves as an eschatological symbol within Tolkien's narrative. It points toward the Catholic hope for a New Heaven and New Earth, where death and sorrow will be no more, held in the promise of eternity with the Divine. Valinor, thus, becomes an earthly foretaste of the heavenly banquet, inviting all to seek the transcendent, the true, and the beautiful.

The role of the Valar in guiding and guarding the destinies of Elves and Men alike reveals a divine council deeply invested in the moral and spiritual development of these races. This involvement is emblematic of the Catholic Church's role in guiding its faithful through the tumult of earthly life toward their ultimate end in God, emphasizing the importance of moral virtue and the constant intercession of the saints on behalf of the world.

The discord sown by Melkor, and the pursuit of remedial justice by the Valar, highlight the perennial battle against evil within Tolkien's mythology, reiterating the Catholic belief in the eventual triumph of good through divine justice. It is a narrative that reinforces the hope in a benevolent, omnipotent, and omniscient God who, though allowing free will, ultimately guides creation toward a good end.

Finally, the tale of the Silmarils and the relentless pursuit of these holy jewels serves as a meditation on the Catholic themes of sacrilege, holiness, and redemption. The Silmarils, as creations filled with the light of the Two Trees, embody the sacred, drawing parallels to Catholic reverence for the divine presence in the sacraments. Their story, marred by treachery and bloodshed, reveals the depths to which creation can fall through sin, yet also holds out the promise of redemption and purification through suffering and sacrifice.

Tolkien's Valinor, with its divine council, presents a world imbued with spiritual depth and moral complexity, reflecting the Catholic vision of creation encompassed by divine providence. The Valar, through their governance, guidance, and guardianship, embody aspects of divine truth that transcend their mythic roles, offering insights into faith, justice, leadership, and the hope of redemption. In studying these narratives, readers find not only escape into fantasy but also a mirror reflecting the truths of their faith, inviting them into a deeper understanding of the divine drama unfolding in their own lives.

In conclusion, "The Valor of Valinor: Understanding the Divine Council" unveils the theological richness woven into the tapestry of Middle-Earth. It serves as a bridge between the fantastical and the spiritual, reminding us that behind the veil of fiction lies a vibrant reflection of divine reality—inviting an exploration of the depths of Catholic doctrine through the lens of Tolkien's mythopoeic universe. This chapter, thus, draws back the curtain on a world where divine valor and virtue illuminate the path toward understanding the mysteries of faith, stewardship, and divine providence.

Melkor's Fall: A Catholic Reading of Evil and Pride

In the grand tapestry of Tolkien's mythopoeic universe, the story of Melkor's descent from the mightiest of the Ainur to the dark lord Morgoth is not merely a tale of cosmic rebellion but a profound reflection on the nature of evil and pride. This narrative, woven with intricate threads of divine providence and free will, invites a Catholic interpretation that resonates deeply with the teachings of the Church. Melkor's fall, far from being an isolated event in the annals of Middle-earth, is emblematic of the primordial struggle between light and darkness, a theme that is thoroughly explored in the rich fabric of Catholic theology.

At the heart of Melkor's tragedy is the sin of pride. It is pride that first stirs in him the desire to create and command, not as a co-creator with Eru Ilúvatar, but in opposition to the divine harmony. This desire for dominion and control, couched in the guise of bringing order and beauty, is a distortion of the natural order. It echoes the teaching of Saint Augustine, who identifies pride as "the beginning of sin" (Augustine, 397). Melkor, in his pride, seeks not to contribute to the Music of the Ainur, but to alter its course to his own design, an act of hubris that leads to his downfall.

Evil, in the Catholic understanding, is not a substance but a privation of good, a corruption of what is inherently good.

Melkor's fall exemplifies this concept. His initial brilliance and power, gifts bestowed upon him by Eru, are perverted by his prideful rebellion. Rather than adding to the beauty of creation, his actions introduce discord. Just as Lucifer's fall from grace in Christian tradition is rooted in pride (Isaiah 14:12-15), so too is Melkor's rebellion a manifestation of the same fatal flaw.

The Catholic reading of Melkor's fall also sheds light on the nature of free will. Tolkien's universe is predicated on the notion that the Ainur, and later the inhabitants of Middle-earth, are endowed with the freedom to choose their paths. This aligns with the Catholic understanding that free will is a gift from God, allowing for the exercise of genuine love and virtue. Yet, with this gift comes the potential for sin. Melkor's choice to rebel against Eru signifies a misuse of free will, a theme that resonates with the story of Adam and Eve's fall in the Garden of Eden.

The consequences of Melkor's fall are far-reaching, affecting not only him but also the fabric of Middle-earth itself. In Catholic thought, the notion of original sin explains how the sin of the first parents brought corruption into the world, a concept mirrored in Tolkien's narrative. The discord sown by Melkor mars the initial perfection of creation, introducing death, suffering, and moral decay. Yet, it is crucial to note that evil is not depicted as equal or coeternal with good. Eru Ilúvatar's foreknowledge and providence ensure that even the discord introduced by Melkor is ultimately woven into a greater harmony.

This divine providence is evident in the way Eru transforms Melkor's malice into opportunities for the emergence of unexpected beauty and heroism. The very existence of the Elves, the Ents, and the noble lineages of Men is in many ways a direct or indirect response to the challenges posed by evil. This reflects the Catholic belief in God's ability to bring good out of evil (cf. Romans 8:28), a central tenet of theodicy, the defense of God's goodness in the face of evil's existence.

Moreover, Melkor's fall and its aftermath offer a meditation on the nature of suffering and sacrifice. The trials faced by the peoples of Middle-earth, particularly in their resistance against Melkor and his successor Sauron, are reminiscent of the Catholic understanding of redemptive suffering. Just as Christ's sacrifice on the cross is a pivotal event for humanity's redemption, so too do the sacrifices made by Elves, Men, and even the humble Hobbits play a critical role in Middle-earth's history.

Finally, the story of Melkor's fall invites reflection on the theme of hope. In Catholic eschatology, the ultimate defeat of evil and the restoration of all things in Christ is a promise that believers cling to. Similarly, in Tolkien's universe, despite the pervasive shadow of Melkor's influence, there remains a steadfast hope in the eventual triumph of good. This hope is not baseless optimism but is grounded in the faithfulness of Eru and the resilience of those who align themselves with the good.

Through the Catholic lens, Melkor's fall is not solely a tale of loss and lamentation but also a narrative rich with theological insights. It invites us to ponder the mysteries of free will, the nature of evil, the role of suffering, and the power of hope. These themes, deeply embedded in Tolkien's mythopoeic universe, challenge us to reflect on our journey, the choices we make, and the hope we profess.

In conclusion, the story of Melkor's fall, as depicted by Tolkien, serves as a profound meditation on the dynamics of evil and pride. Its parallels with Catholic thought offer a rich vein of theological reflection, inviting readers to explore the depths of both Tolkien's creation and their faith. Melkor's fall, while a cautionary tale, also illuminates the path toward understanding, redemption, and ultimately, hope in the face of darkness.

The Role of The Valkyries: Guardianship and Divine Will In exploring the vast cosmos Tolkien has created, we encounter a multitude of characters and beings, each with their unique role and purpose within the narrative's theological tapestry. Among these are the Valkyries, ethereal yet formidable entities, whose portrayal and purpose resonate with themes of guardianship and divine will, thus opening a dialogue with Roman Catholic doctrine concerning providence and the stewardship of creation.

The concept of the Valkyries, though rooted in Norse mythology, is reimagined by Tolkien to embody principles that align closely with Catholic teachings on angels. As guardians, their role transcends mere martial prowess; they are caretakers of divine order and executors of the will of Eru Ilúvatar, Tolkien's equivalent of God in his legendarium. This alignment with a higher divine will mirrors the Catholic understanding of angels as God's messengers and servants, tasked with the protection and guidance of humanity (CCC, 331).

Within the structure of Middle-Earth, the Valkyries serve as a bridge between the earthly and the divine, mediating the divine will and manifesting it in ways that are crucial for the unfolding of the world's history. This is akin to the Catholic concept of Providence, wherein God guides creation towards its ultimate good and fulfillment, often through intermediary agents (CCC, 302-303).

Their guardianship is portrayed not as a dominion over those they protect but as a service, a theme deeply resonant with the Catholic ethos of servant leadership (John 13:12-14). This humble guardianship is a mark of their alignment with the divine will, as they seek not their own glory but the fulfillment of the purpose for which they were created.

Significantly, the Valkyries' selection of those who die in battle and those who live harks back to the theological theme of divine election. However, unlike predestinarian doctrines, this choice is portrayed as depending on the valor and virtue of the individuals in question. This reflects a nuanced Catholic understanding of predestination, where divine foreknowledge and human free will coexist in a mysterious harmony (CCC, 600).

The presence and actions of the Valkyries within the narrative often herald moments of pivotal change and eucatastrophic turns. These moments can be seen as manifestations of what Tolkien termed the 'eucatastrophe', a sudden and favorable resolution of events in a story, symbolizing the Catholic doctrine of hope and the belief in a benevolent Providence guiding the universe towards its ultimate redemption (1 Peter 1:6-7).

Their discernment in choosing the fallen is emblematic of the eschatological theme of judgment, another area where Tolkien's work dialogues with Catholic theology. The Valkyries, in their capacity as selectors of the slain, echo the Christian belief in a particular judgment, where souls are assessed at the time of death, determining their fate in the afterlife (CCC, 1021-1022).

Furthermore, their dual role as warriors and weavers of fate introduces a paradox; they embody the inevitability of death and the valor in facing it. This duality invites reflection on Catholic teachings regarding the nature of suffering and death as not merely an end but a passage into a new form of existence in God's eternal design (CCC, 1010).

In their silence and mystery, the Valkyries also embody the ineffability of God's ways. While their choices may sometimes appear arbitrary or inscrutable, they act within the bounds of divine wisdom, a reminder of the Catholic trust in God's inscrutable but always merciful judgment (Romans 11:33-34).

Operating beyond the bounds of time, the Valkyries' perspective is eternal, symbolizing the idea that divine providence encompasses all of history, from creation to eschaton. This eternal viewpoint encourages a contemplation of salvation history as a continuous unfolding of God's will, guided by divine foresight and love (CCC, 323).

Their existence suggests a cosmology where multiple orders of being coalesce to fulfill divine will, resonating with the Catholic vision of the universe as a hierarchy of creatures, spiritual and corporeal, serving God's plan (CCC, 325).

This tapestry of themes — guardianship, divine will, judgment, and hope — woven through the narrative role of the Valkyries, reflects a profound engagement with Catholic theological concepts. Through their actions and the themes they embody, the Valkyries contribute to a richer understanding of the divine economy of salvation as depicted in Tolkien's mythology.

As intermediaries between the divine and the mortal, the Valkyries serve a function analogous to that of the saints and angels in Catholic tradition. They remind us that the divine will operates through the agency of created beings, within the grand narrative of salvation history, pointing towards the ultimate reconciliation of all things in Christ (Colossians 1:20).

Thus, studying the role of the Valkyries within Tolkien's legendarium offers a unique lens through which to explore and elucidate Roman Catholic doctrine on creation, providence, and eschatology. It reveals how mythology, far from being mere fantasy, can serve as a profound medium for theological reflection and dialogue.

In conclusion, the Valkyries, as depicted by Tolkien, encapsulate themes of guardianship and divine will that resonate deeply with Catholic theological traditions. Their portrayal offers not only a fascinating aspect of Middle-Earth's mythopoeic tapestry but also a rich avenue for exploring the intersections of faith, storytelling, and the enduring human quest for meaning in the cosmos.

Chapter 3: Men, Elves, and Free Will: A Catholic Dialogue

The discourse on free will within the confines of Middle-Earth, especially in the context of Men and Elves, opens an illuminating pathway to understanding Catholic teachings on creation and providence. While the Elves embody the aspect of an immortal creation tied intrinsically to the fate of the world itself, Men bear the 'Gift of Men,' a notion enshrined in both mortality and the freedom to shape their destinies unbound to the world's end. This duality presents a compelling dialogue with Catholic understanding of free will, bestowed by an omnipotent, benevolent God.

At the heart of this conversation is the assertion of free will as a gift from the Creator, allowing for the manifestation of love, virtue, and communion with the Divine. In the framework of Tolkien's universe, Elves, with their undying nature, represent a form of pre-lapsarian innocence, yet their fates are tightly interwoven with the physical world, limiting their capacity to transcend it. In contrast, Men's mortality, a seeming limitation, grants them an autonomy in alignment with Catholic views on free will and the human ability to choose their ultimate destiny.

The juxtaposition of Elf and Man reveals a nuanced theological narrative. Tolkien, through these races, navigates the complexities of free will, providence, and destiny, paralleling the

Catholic vision of life as a journey towards God, marked by choices that either estrange or draw one closer to the Divine. The Elves' eternal bond with Arda signifies a predetermined path, restricting their ability to fully exercise free will in a Catholic sense, as their actions, though free, are ultimately subservient to the world's fate.

Conversely, the Gift of Men, while initially perceived as a curse of mortality, emerges as a profound blessing enabling humans to forge paths independent of the world's physical and temporal confines. This gift aligns with the Catholic understanding of life's transitory nature and the primacy of spiritual over material existence. It underscores a freedom that, though bounded by the consequences of sin—echoing the Fall—is also a pathway to redemption and communion with the Divine, achievable through grace and the exercise of free will toward good.

The narrative of Elves and Men in Tolkien's Middle-Earth serves as an allegory to the Catholic teachings on free will and providence. For as Augustine posited, true freedom is not the absence of constraints but the ability to choose the good (Augustine, 397). This theological underpinning finds resonance in the choices made by Tolkien's characters, whether elf or man, each exercising free will within the bounds of their creation, yet striving towards a goodness that transcends the immediate.

The divine providence in Tolkien's work, manifest in the overarching narrative that guides Middle-Earth towards an ultimate eucatastrophe, parallels Catholic understanding of God's providential care. It is a providence that does not negate free will but, instead, encompasses it, guiding creation towards an ultimate good without stripping the individual of autonomy. This delicate balance forms the crux of the Catholic dialogue with Tolkien's fictional universe, revealing the complementarity of free will and divine providence.

Furthermore, the theme of sacrifice, evident in the narratives of both Elves and Men, underlines the Catholic ethos of self-giving love. Characters from both races are seen making monumental sacrifices, underwritten by their exercise of free will for a greater good. These acts of sacrifice illuminate the Catholic understanding of love's sacrificial nature, mirroring the ultimate sacrifice of Christ.

In conclusion, the exploration of Men, Elves, and free will within Tolkien's lore offers a rich tapestry for dialoguing with Catholic doctrine. It brings to the fore the complexities and beauties of creation, the profound nature of free will, and the hopeful assurance of providence. While navigating a world of myth and legend, this dialogue uncovers timeless truths about the human condition, divine love, and the journey towards ultimate goodness.

In understanding these allegorical representations, the reader is invited to reflect upon their own exercise of free will within the providential plan of a loving Creator. Thus, Tolkien's Middle-Earth, with its intricate portrayal of Men, Elves, and their destinies, can be seen as a profound meditation on the Catholic faith, offering insights into the mysteries of freedom, sacrifice, and divine love.

The Gift of Men: Death and Immortality in a Catholic Context

In the broad tapestry woven by J.R.R. Tolkien in his creation myth and subsequent tales of Middle-Earth, few themes resonate as profoundly with Catholic teaching as the concepts of death and immortality. These motifs, especially as they pertain to the differing fates of Elves and Men, offer a rich field for dialogue with Catholic eschatology and anthropology.

Elves, in Tolkien's universe, are bound to the world for its duration, their fate inseparably linked to the very essence of Arda. Their immortality is a double-edged sword, granting them an endless expanse of days yet also a deepening acquaintance with sorrow as they witness the cycles of growth and decay, of building up and breaking down. This eternal perspective on the world is akin to the nature of angels within Catholic theology, beings outside the limits of human temporality. However, unlike angels, Elves are still corporeal beings, deeply tied to the material world and its fate.

Men, on the other hand, are bestowed with what Tolkien termed the 'Gift of Men': death. This gift, though often viewed through a lens darkened by grief and fear, holds a deeper theological significance within both Tolkien's subcreation and the Catholic understanding of human destiny. Death is not merely an end but a liberation, a passage from the temporal into the eternal, from the confines of a fallen world into the possibility of direct communion with the Divine.

At first glance, the mortality of Men in Tolkien's mythology may seem a curse when contrasted with the seemingly enviable immortal existence of the Elves. Yet, it's precisely through this gift that Men are offered something Elves desire but cannot attain: the ability to escape the circles of the world, to transcend the material and participate in a destiny beyond Arda. This echoes the Catholic teaching that human mortality opens the door to union with God in a way that worldly immortality cannot.

The longing of the Elves for the death they cannot have, as evidenced in their songs and tales, mirrors the human longing for transcendence, for a reality beyond the limits of our mortal existence. The Elves' lament, in its deepest essence, is a reflection of the human condition, a recognition of the inherent limitations of a purely immanent existence and a yearning for the transcendent, for communion with the Absolute.

In the Catholic tradition, death is understood as a consequence of original sin yet also as a means of grace, an opportunity for ultimate communion with God through Christ's redemptive death and resurrection. In a similar vein, Tolkien imbues the death of Men with a redemptive and hopeful aspect, framing it as a divine gift rather than a punishment.

The Valar's bewilderment at the Gift of Men underscores a significant thematic point: the limitations of even the most powerful beings within the created order to fully comprehend the divine plan. It speaks to the mystery of God's providence in Catholic thought, which holds that divine wisdom and purposes, especially concerning life and death, are often beyond human understanding.

Furthermore, the story of Númenor, with its tragic quest for immortality and the subsequent downfall, serves as a stark illustration of the perils of rejecting one's mortal nature. This narrative resonates with the Catholic caution against the hubris of seeking to overcome the natural order established by God, emphasizing instead a humble acceptance of human limits and mortality.

The eventual departure of the Elves from Middle-Earth, making way for the Dominion of Men, symbolizes a transition from the mythic to the historical, from an immortal race bound to the fate of the material world to a mortal race with a destiny that lies beyond it. This transition can be seen as a metaphor for the Christian understanding of history as moving towards a telos, an ultimate fulfillment that transcends the temporal realm.

At the heart of Tolkien's portrayal of Men and Elves lies a fundamental optimism about the human condition: through the Gift of Men, mortality becomes not a limit but a liberation, not an end but a beginning. This perspective offers a powerful affirmation of the Catholic view of death and salvation, emphasizing the hope and potential inherent in the human experience.

In conclusion, Tolkien's nuanced exploration of death and immortality, embodied in the destinies of Elves and Men, provides a fertile ground for engaging with Catholic doctrine. It reaffirms the belief in a divine providence that directs us, through the passage of death, towards an encounter with the eternal, highlighting the profound dignity and purpose bestowed upon humanity by the Creator.

This dialogue between Tolkien's mythology and Catholic theology enriches our understanding of both, opening up new dimensions of meaning in the themes of death, immortality, and the human quest for transcendence. By exploring these themes through the lens of faith, we see the Gift of Men not as a lamentable fate but as a hopeful promise, a divine invitation to partake in the mystery of everlasting life.

In the previous chapters, we've delved into the intricacies of Tolkien's universe, exploring the divine hierarchy and the role of free will in the fate of Elves and Men alike. This meticulous groundwork paves the way for a profound comparative analysis between Elvish immortality and human destiny, realms deeply intertwined with Catholic doctrine and eschatological beliefs. **Elvish Immortality and Human Destiny: A Comparative Analysis** seeks to bridge the gap between Tolkien's mythic creation and Catholic theological perspectives.

At the heart of Tolkien's universe lies the distinction between Elves and Men, immortal beings bound to the world until its end and mortal beings bestowed with the Gift of Men - death. This fundamental separation unveils diverse paths of existence and destinies within the created order, mirroring the intricate Catholic contemplation on the nature of the soul, immortality, and the afterlife.

Elves, in their eternal bond with the world, experience a continuity of being that allows for a deep accumulation of wisdom and knowledge. Their immortality, however, is a double-edged sword. It subjects them to the weariness of the world, a concept analogous to the spiritual desolation that can afflict the most devout souls in their earthly pilgrimage. Just as the Elves yearn for the undying lands of the West, so does the human soul long for the beatific vision, the ultimate communion with the Divine beyond the temporal realm.

Men, on the other hand, bear a mysterious gift from Ilúvatar - death, which Tolkien, through a Catholic lens, interprets as liberation from the confines of the world and an entryway to a union with the Divine. This dichotomy between Elf and Man reflects the Christian understanding of earthly life as a preparation for the hereafter, where eternal destiny unfolds.

The philosophical underpinnings of Tolkien's narrative resonate with the Catholic teaching on the soul's immortality and its consequential journey post death. While Elves represent an unending earthly journey akin to the angels' immortal existence, Men's destinies align with the Christian eschatological vision - a transient life on earth followed by an eternal life either in communion with God or in separation from Him.

This distinction also delves into the nature of free will and its implications for both Elves and Men. Elves, despite their immortality, are not free from the consequences of their actions; their history is rife with tragedy stemming from pride and desire for power. This narrative mirrors the Catholic understanding of sin and its repercussions, emphasizing the moral responsibility that comes with free will.

Men's transitory nature, infused with the gift of death, offers a unique perspective on the value of time and the urgency of moral decisions. The fleetingness of human life serves as a catalyst for reflection on one's actions and their eternal implications, a thematic element deeply rooted in Catholic eschatological thought.

The role of providence in Tolkien's world further encapsulates the theological dialogue between predestination and free will. Both Elves and Men operate within the boundaries of Ilúvatar's overarching plan, yet their autonomy allows for the unfolding of personal and collective destinies in complex and often unexpected ways. This dynamic interplay reflects the Catholic view of divine providence, which upholds God's ultimate plan while honoring human freedom.

The eventual fading of the Elves from Middle-Earth signals the passing of an ancient order, making way for the Age of Men. This transition can be interpreted through a Catholic lens as the movement from the Old Covenant, characterized by law and prophecy, to the New Covenant, marked by grace and fulfillment in Christ. The dominion of Men symbolizes a new phase in the divine economy, where the temporal is increasingly infused with the spiritual, leading toward ultimate redemption.

Yet, the concept of elves sailing to Valinor, a realm beyond the normal confines of the world, introduces an eschatological dimension that parallels Catholic notions of purgatory, heaven, and paradise. Valinor is not merely a place but a state of being that represents the fulfillment of longing, the healing of wounds, and the completion of existence in a way that resonates with the Christian hope of heaven.

In the grand tapestry of Tolkien's mythology, the interplay between Elvish immortality and human destiny encapsulates a profound theological reflection on life, death, and the afterlife. Through the lens of Catholic doctrine, these themes acquire an added depth, inviting readers to contemplate the mysteries of existence, the nature of the soul, and the promise of eternal life.

Ultimately, Tolkien's portrayal of Elves and Men offers a rich narrative framework for exploring Catholic teachings on creation, the nature of the soul, and eschatology. This comparative analysis reveals the depth of Tolkien's theological imagination, inviting readers to reflect on their own destinies in light of divine providence and the eschatological promises that lie at the heart of Catholic faith.

As we journey through Middle-Earth, traversing the ageless forests with the Elves or marching toward uncertain fates with Men, we are reminded of the enduring human quest for meaning, the longing for transcendence, and the hope of eternal communion with the Divine. In embracing these themes, Tolkien's work becomes not only a mirror reflecting theological truths but also a gateway to deeper spiritual contemplation and understanding.

Thus, in the comparative analysis of Elvish immortality and human destiny, we find a confluence of myth and theology, imagination and doctrine, inviting us to explore the labyrinthine paths of faith and fantasy. Through this exploration, the distinctions and parallels between the fates of Elves and Men illuminate the broader tapestry of Catholic eschatology, enriching our understanding of the divine plan and our place within it.

References:

Chapter 4: Divine Purpose in the Struggles of Middle-Earth

Within the fabric of Middle-Earth, woven through its tumultuous histories and the heart-wrenching narratives of its denizens, lies a thread of divine purpose. This purpose, while not always immediately apparent to the characters within J.R.R. Tolkien's legendarium, underscores a deeper theological dialogue with the nature of providence. Providence, in the Roman Catholic understanding, is the means through which God's ultimate plan is unfurled in creation, despite—or perhaps through—the presence of evil and suffering.

The struggles faced by the myriad races of Middle-Earth are not merely tales of heroism and valor but are imbued with a deeper significance through the lens of Catholic doctrine. Each trial, each seemingly insurmountable ordeal, becomes a crucible through which the divine purpose is both revealed and realized. The characters' journeys across the landscapes of Tolkien's imagination become emblematic of the spiritual journey undertaken by all believers, a pilgrimage through the darkness of a fallen world towards the light of divine grace.

Central to understanding the divine purpose within these struggles is the concept of the eucatastrophe, a term coined by Tolkien himself. This concept, representing a sudden turn of events that leads to the protagonist's salvation, echoes the

Catholic belief in hope and redemption through divine intervention. It embodies the theological assertion that God's plan ultimately culminates in the good, despite the convolutions of individual narratives marked by sin and downfall.

In the plight of Frodo, an unassuming hobbit tasked with an overwhelming burden, one can discern the interplay of free will and providence. His journey underscores not only the power of individual choice in the face of evil but also how these choices align with a greater divine orchestration. Frodo's perseverance, supported by the fellowship around him, becomes a metaphor for the communal aspect of salvation and the belief that grace often operates through the bonds of fellowship and love.

The conflict between the forces of Melkor and the free peoples of Middle-Earth serves as a backdrop to explore the nature of evil and its place within divine providence. Evil, as depicted through Melkor's rebellion and the subsequent fall from grace, is not an absence of good but a corruption of it. This understanding mirrors Catholic teachings regarding the origin of evil and its role in the narrative of salvation history, wherein evil, through divine omnipotence, is ultimately used to bring about a greater good.

Moreover, the ethos of the Valar, especially in their guardianship of creation and their opposition to Melkor, illuminates the

Catholic doctrine of the communion of saints and angels. The Valar's interventions in the history of Middle-Earth, though subtle and often indirect, reflect the belief in a celestial hierarchy working in concert with divine will to guide and protect the faithful.

Another poignant illustration of divine purpose is witnessed in the eschatological imagery present within Tolkien's oeuvre. The eventual victory over Sauron and the restoration of peace to Middle-Earth serve as a foretaste of the Catholic anticipation of a new creation, where evil is vanquished, and divine harmony is restored. This culmination of history within the narrative world of Middle-Earth mirrors the eschatological hope inherent in Catholic theology, a hope firmly anchored in the promise of divine justice and mercy.

It is through these thematic elements—providence, free will, the nature of evil, and eschatological hope—that Tolkien's mythopoeic vision aligns with and elucidates Catholic doctrine. The divine purpose in the struggles of Middle-Earth, while manifested through fantastical narratives and mythical beings, resonates deeply with the theological convictions regarding the presence of the divine in human history, the role of free will in the economy of salvation, and the ultimate victory of good over evil.

In conclusion, the struggles of Middle-Earth, far from being mere vehicles for adventure and fantasy, are imbued with a profound theological significance. They invite the reader to reflect on the presence of divine purpose in the midst of suffering and the inexorable movement of creation towards its ultimate redemption. Through the lens of Catholic doctrine, the tales of Middle-Earth become not only narratives of high fantasy but also profound meditations on the nature of providence, the power of free will, and the promise of eschatological fulfillment.

Tolkien's Catholic Vision of Providence: Trust in the Eucatastrophe

In the vast expanse of narrative and myth that J.R.R. Tolkien has bestowed upon our world, there lies embedded a deeply Catholic vision of providence, one that beckons its readers towards a trust in what Tolkien himself termed the 'eucatastrophe'. This notion, essentially the 'good catastrophe', illustrates a fundamental theological concept wherein, amid the greatest despair, hope is to be found not outside of, but through divine intervention.

Tolkien's Middle-Earth, wrought with peril and shadowed in moments by sheer hopelessness, reveals through its unfolding a tapestry of divine providence. The characters within, each carrying their burden, are led not merely by fate but by a guided hand that moves unseen. This vision, inherently Catholic in its nuances, imbues the narrative with layers that transcend mere storytelling.

The eucatastrophe emerges as a beacon of trust, a sudden and unexpected turn towards salvation in the narrative of Middle-Earth. For Tolkien, this was not merely a literary device, but a reflection of the world's ultimate Truth. It's an assertion that no matter the depth of darkness, a light, often unforeseen, breaks through — symbolizing the Catholic understanding of grace and divine intervention.

In discussing this Catholic vision, it's crucial to perceive the craftsmanship with which Tolkien wove providence into his narratives. Each character's journey, fraught with choices both free and coerced, mirrors the Catholic teaching on free will and its dance with destiny. The providence that Tolkien illustrates is not a puppeteer's string but a gentle guiding, a whisper in the heart of his characters leading them to their eucatastrophe.

This trust in providence is epitomized in the journey of Frodo and Sam. Against insurmountable odds, their path is beset with moments of grace that carry them forward. These instances, small and grand, encapsulate Tolkien's conviction that providence is intricately involved in the details of life, guiding towards a greater good.

The concept of the eucatastrophe is steeped in Catholic eschatology, which holds that history moves towards a divine fulfillment. Tolkien's narratives, while not allegorical, are imbued with this sense of ultimate hope. This eschatological vision ensures that the darkness of Middle-Earth is not final, and that, in the grand tale of creation, all shall be made well.

This vision is profoundly sacramental, seeing the material world as a channel of divine grace. Middle-Earth, with its sacred places and enchanted objects, serves almost as a sacramental cosmos, where the physical and the spiritual intersect continually. This Catholic perception bridges the seen with the unseen, suggesting that the material world, while fallen, remains a vessel for divine grace.

The trust in the eucatastrophe also embodies a profoundly Catholic understanding of suffering. In Tolkien's Middle-Earth, suffering is never meaningless but is often the very means by which providence operates. This aligns with the Catholic belief in the redemptive nature of suffering, a concept that sees in every struggle a potential moment for divine grace to manifest, leading to a greater good.

This narrative structure is not a mere call to passive hope but an invocation to active trust. The characters in Middle-Earth, while often unaware of the full scope of their role, embrace their journey with a fidelity that reflects the Catholic call to faith. Their trust in the face of darkness, their hope against despair, are testaments to the providential vision that undergirds Tolkien's work.

Understanding Tolkien's eucatastrophic vision offers a new lens through which to engage with his oeuvre. It reveals the depth of his Catholic faith and how it permeated his storytelling. Middle-Earth becomes more than a mythical land; it becomes a narrative theology that speaks profoundly to the human condition.

This vision of providence and eucatastrophe resonates with a universal human experience. It acknowledges the coexistence of suffering and hope, of free will and divine guidance. It's a testament to the power of story to convey profound truths about life, faith, and the ultimate good.

In a world often overshadowed by cynicism and despair, Tolkien's narrative offers a counter-narrative, one steeped in the Catholic tradition but universal in its appeal. It calls for a trust in the eucatastrophe, a belief in eventual good, not as naiveté but as a profound act of faith in divine providence.

Tolkien's works, then, serve not only as a source of literary pleasure but as a profound meditation on the nature of providence, free will, and the ultimate triumph of good. Through his Catholic vision, he invites readers to see the world, with all its shadows, as still under the guiding hand of a benevolent creator.

This vision of Middle-Earth, rich in its theological implications, offers a unique opportunity for dialogue between faith and literature. It opens pathways for understanding divine providence not just as a theological concept but as a lived reality, intricately woven into the fabric of both Middle-Earth and our own world.

In conclusion, Tolkien's Catholic vision of providence, manifest in his trust in the eucatastrophe, reflects a deeply held belief in the ultimate goodness that lies beyond the apparent chaos of the world. It's a vision that not only enriches our reading of his works but also invites us to trust in the greater narrative of divine providence in our own lives.

Frodo's Journey: Providence and Free Will Intertwined

In the vast and rich tapestry of Middle-earth, woven with threads of myth and legend by J.R.R. Tolkien, few tales possess as profound a theological resonance as the journey of Frodo Baggins. This small, unlikely hero's quest to destroy the One Ring is not just a narrative of good versus evil but a deeply textured exploration of providence and free will, themes central to Roman Catholic theology. The interplay of these elements in Frodo's journey offers a fertile ground for reflection on the nature of godly providence, human freedom, and their role in the unfolding of divine purposes.

Frodo Baggins, a hobbit of the Shire, is thrust into an epic adventure, bearing the burden of the One Ring with a mission to destroy it in the fires of Mount Doom. His journey is emblematic of every soul's pilgrimage through life, marked by choices, challenges, and the overarching guidance of providence. The Catholic tradition holds that God, in His omniscience, omnipotence, and omnipresence, orchestrates everything towards an ultimate good, yet without infringing on the creature's free will. Frodo's free acceptance of his role as the Ring-bearer parallels this belief, illustrating how divine providence doesn't negate human freedom but rather presupposes and uplifts it.

Throughout his quest, Frodo encounters numerous instances where chance—or what might better be termed providence—guides his steps. From his narrow escapes from the Black Riders to the serendipitous meeting with Gollum, who plays a crucial role in the Ring's destruction, Frodo's path seems steered by an unseen hand. Yet, at each juncture, Frodo's choices remain vitally his own. He decides to press on, to trust, to show mercy. This dance between destiny and decision captures the essence of Tolkien's Catholic perspective: God's will operates alongside human action, not overriding it but mysteriously integrating it into a larger divine narrative.

The character of Frodo also embodies the Christian understanding of suffering and sacrifice. Carrying the Ring, a symbol of sin and its burdens, Frodo experiences a profound inner agony akin to Christ's passion. His wounds, both physical and spiritual, are the price of his sacrificial love, a love that participates in the redemptive suffering of Christ. Through this lens, Frodo's journey is a meditation on the mystery of suffering: a journey through which divine providence brings about a greater good from the depths of despair and sacrifice.

Moreover, Frodo's reliance on fellowship mirrors the Catholic emphasis on the communal aspect of salvation. Though chosen for a singular task, Frodo is accompanied by companions who support and aid him, reflecting the Christian belief in the Church as the mystical body of Christ. In this communal journey, the free will of each member contributes to the fulfillment of their shared destiny, underlining how individual freedom and divine providence coalesce within the context of community.

The intricate relationship between providence and free will is further highlighted in Frodo's interactions with Gollum. Despite Gollum's treachery, Frodo extends mercy, a decision that is crucial to the Ring's eventual destruction. This act of forgiveness underscores the Catholic teaching that grace can work through our free responses to God's call, turning even our failures and the malice of others towards the fulfillment of His plan. Frodo's mercy, therefore, becomes an instrumental part of providence's unfolding narrative.

In the end, Frodo's journey transcends a mere physical odyssey to Mount Doom; it becomes a spiritual pilgrimage towards understanding and accepting divine will. The resolution of his quest, marked by apparent chance but guided by providence, reaffirms the Catholic doctrine that God brings about His purposes through the tapestry of human freedom and choice. Frodo's story, in its complexity and depth, becomes a powerful allegory for the mysterious interplay of free will and divine guidance in our lives.

As we reflect on Frodo's journey, it becomes clear that Tolkien's mythopoeic universe, while fictional, offers profound insights into the workings of providence and the dignity of free will. It challenges us to see our own lives as part of a grander narrative, one in which our choices matter deeply, yet are held within the embrace of divine providence. In this way, Tolkien, through the story of a small hobbit from the Shire, illuminates the path of faith: a path marked by freedom, guided by love, and leading towards the ultimate Good.

In conclusion, Frodo's journey in "The Lord of the Rings" serves not merely as an epic tale of adventure and conflict but as a profound theological discourse on providence and free will. This narrative beautifully intertwines human freedom with divine orchestration, reflecting the Catholic understanding of a God who is intimately involved in the tapestry of creation, steering it gently yet decisively towards its eschatological fulfillment. Thus, Frodo's story becomes a microcosm of the universal tale of salvation history, a tale in which each soul plays a part, guided by the provident hand of God yet moving freely towards its destined end.

References:

The Theology of Hope: Eschatology in The Lord of the Rings

In the tapestry of Middle-Earth, J.R.R. Tolkien weaves a narrative deeply imbued with eschatological themes, presenting a world in which the fruition of hope is not merely a wish but an eminent promise. This chapter delves into the profound implications of eschatology within "The Lord of the Rings," exploring how Tolkien's Catholic imagination informs the culmination of hope through the lens of divine providence and the ultimate fulfillment of the world's destiny.

At its core, eschatology in Tolkien's epic saga is encapsulated in the anticipation of the inevitable defeat of evil and the restoration of the world. The pivotal point of this hope is epitomized in the return of King Elessar, an event that mirrors the Catholic expectation of the Second Coming. Through Aragorn's crowning, Tolkien illustrates not only the restoration of the kingdom of Gondor but also hints at a larger, cosmic restoration of harmony and order, a theme central to Catholic eschatological belief. This restoration signifies the hope for a new world where peace prevails over warfare, and harmony displaces discord.

Embedded within the narrative is the character of Samwise Gamgee, whose journey embodies the essence of apostolic hope. Sam's unwavering faith in the fulfillment of Frodo's mission and the inherent goodness of the world serves as a beacon to readers. His resilience in the face of despair and his ability to find light in the darkest of times are emblematic of the theological virtue of hope. Samwise, in his modesty and bravery, aligns with the Catholic understanding of being a witness to hope amidst adversity.

The overarching narrative of "The Lord of the Rings" suggests that hope is not a passive waiting but an active engagement in the struggle against evil. This aligns with the Catholic view that hope in the eschatological promise requires participation in the realization of that promise. The characters' endeavors, fraught with peril and sacrifice, underscore the belief that hope is forged in the crucible of trials. Their journey reveals that hope, when anchored in faith, has the power to overcome even the mightiest of adversities.

Furthermore, Tolkien's portrayal of the destruction of the Ring in Mount Doom serves as a metaphor for the Catholic concept of purgatory, where purification occurs before the soul can enter into the fullness of its eschatological hope. The fiery chasm into which the Ring falls becomes a place of both ending and renewal, symbolizing the eschatological belief in a new creation that emerges from the purging of the old.

The eschatological vision presented in Tolkien's work is inherently linked to the theme of divine providence. It suggests that the unfolding of history and the eventual triumph of good over evil are underpinned by a providential design. This divine guidance assures readers that despite the apparent dominance of darkness, a benevolent plan is at work, steering the world towards its destined end.

"The Lord of the Rings" encapsulates the journey towards an eschatological hope that resonates deeply with Catholic eschatology. It depicts a world where the forces of good, guided by providence, engage in a cosmic battle against the forces of evil. This struggle, while fraught with despair and seeming defeat, ultimately affirms the power of hope to illuminate the darkest corners of existence.

In conclusion, the eschatological themes woven into the fabric of "The Lord of the Rings" offer a rich tapestry for understanding the complexities of hope, providence, and the ultimate fulfillment of the world's destiny from a Catholic perspective. Tolkien's masterpiece serves not only as a compelling narrative of fantasy but also as a profound meditation on the theological virtue of hope and its significance in the world.

References:

Carpenter, H. (2000). J.R.R. Tolkien: A Biography. Allen & Unwin.

Flieger, V. (2002). Splintered Light: Logos and Language in Tolkien's World. Kent State University Press.

Shippey, T. (2001). J.R.R. Tolkien: Author of the Century. HarperCollins.

The Return of the King: Catholic Symbolism and the Second Coming

In the sweeping epic of *The Lord of the Rings*, J.R.R. Tolkien weaves an intricate tapestry of symbolism and narrative that draws heavily upon his Catholic faith. Among the most profound and significant of these elements is the portrayal of the return of the king, an event that mirrors the eschatological hope found in Catholic theology concerning the Second Coming of Christ. This chapter seeks to unravel these layers of meaning, exploring how Tolkien's work not only depicts a battle between good and evil but also encapsulates a deeply theological vision of history, hope, and redemption.

At the heart of Tolkien's narrative is the figure of Aragorn, the true king whose return is long foretold and eagerly awaited by the people of Middle-earth. In Catholic eschatology, the theme of waiting and preparation for the Second Coming is paramount. It is a period marked by vigilance, prayer, and penance, reflecting a deep yearning for the fulfillment of God's kingdom. Similarly, in Middle-earth, the anticipation of Aragorn's return symbolizes a deeper hope among the Free Peoples for renewal and restoration.

The concept of kingship in Tolkien's work is imbued with rich sacramental and Christological significance. Aragorn, as the returning king, serves as a Christ-figure, embodying virtues that reflect the Kingship of Christ—justice, mercy, wisdom, and humility. His journey from exile to his eventual ascension to the throne mirrors the Paschal Mystery of Christ, encompassing themes of suffering, death, and resurrection. Aragorn's healing hands, which bring restoration and peace to the kingdom, further accentuate this Christological parallel, echoing the healing ministry of Jesus.

The climactic event of Aragorn's coronation and his entry into Minas Tirith resonate with the imagery of the triumphant entry of Christ into Jerusalem. It heralds a new era of peace and justice, a fulfillment of prophecy that brings hope and joy to the people. This moment in the narrative can be seen as a foretaste of the promised Parousia, the glorious return of Christ, which will inaugurate the definitive establishment of God's kingdom.

Central to Catholic eschatology is the belief in the Resurrection of the dead and the life of the world to come. Tolkien's legendarium is rife with themes of death and resurrection, not merely as a cessation of life but as a passage to a more profound existence. The defeat of Sauron and the destruction of the Ring lead not only to the restoration of the external order but also signify the restoration of internal order within the hearts of the characters and the land itself—a new creation that echoes the new heaven and new earth promised in Revelation.

The journey of Frodo, as a bearer of the Ring, encapsulates the Christian understanding of carrying one's cross. His mission is one of self-sacrifice, bearing the weight of evil with the hope of its ultimate defeat. This act of self-giving love is at the core of Christian soteriology, where salvation is achieved through the cross—a theme Tolkien masterfully embeds within the fabric of his narrative.

The role of the community in supporting Frodo on his quest mirrors the Church's mission in nurturing and sustaining the faithful as they await the Lord's return. The Fellowship, a communion of different peoples and races, signifies the universal call to unity in the body of Christ, working together for the common good and the establishment of peace.

The eschatological hope in *The Lord of the Rings* is also evident in the portrayal of evil's defeat. Sauron's fall signifies the ultimate victory over sin and death promised in Christian doctrine—a victory achieved through humility, sacrifice, and the small, often unnoticed acts of courage and love. This vision aligns with the Catholic understanding that the Last Judgment will reveal the triumph of God's justice and mercy.

The imagery of light and darkness throughout the saga serves as a powerful metaphor for the Christian narrative of salvation history. The struggle against the shadow reflects the spiritual battle between good and evil, while the eventual triumph of light heralds the coming of the Kingdom of God, where darkness will be no more.

In conclusion, The Return of the King, as depicted in Tolkien's epic, is laden with Catholic symbolism that goes beyond mere allegory to embody a profound theological vision. It speaks to the eschatological hope that is central to the Christian faith—the hope for the return of Christ, the King of Kings, who will bring about the final victory over evil and the restoration of all things. Tolkien's narrative, steeped in the richness of Catholic theology, invites readers to reflect on the deeper realities of our existence, the nature of our longing for redemption, and the promise of a future where peace and justice reign eternal.

Samwise the Faithful: Apostle of Hope

In the grand tapestry of Middle-Earth, interwoven with diverse threads of lore and legend, the humble figure of Samwise Gamgee emerges as a beacon of unwavering fidelity and hope. This chapter delves into the quintessential role of Samwise, not merely as a loyal companion, but as an exemplar of hope, a virtue deeply embedded in the Catholic faith. Samwise's journey alongside Frodo in their perilous quest to destroy the One Ring embodies the theological virtues of faith, hope, and charity, with a pronounced emphasis on hope as the sustaining force in the face of despair.

Hope, in Catholic theology, is not a mere wish for a favorable outcome but a steadfast trust in God's providence and the promise of salvation. Samwise's character manifests this hope through his unshakeable belief in the goodness that persists in the world, even when such belief seems unfounded by the surrounding darkness. His actions, driven by loyalty and love, transcend the bounds of his humble origins, illustrating that hope rooted in faith has the power to challenge and overcome even the most formidable forces of evil.

The narrative arc of Samwise, analyzed through a Catholic lens, echoes the journey of the human soul towards God. Like many biblical figures who faced trials and tribulations with hope,

Samwise's endurance is fueled not by the certainty of success but by the conviction that his actions are aligned with a higher purpose. His resilience serves as a testament to the notion that hope, when anchored in divine truth, becomes an indestructible force that propels individuals beyond their perceived limitations.

Samwise's relationship with Frodo also embodies the sacramental aspect of Christian companionship, wherein two or more gather in mutual support and love, reflecting the presence of Christ among them. In their darkest moments, it is Sam's hope and unwavering commitment that carries Frodo when he can no longer bear the physical and spiritual burden of the Ring. This mirrors the Catholic understanding of bearing one another's burdens, living in communion as a manifestation of God's grace.

Furthermore, Samwise's vision of the world, imbued with wonder and gratitude, showcases the Catholic appreciation for creation as a gift from God. His awe in the face of beauty, even amidst desolation, highlights the sacramental view of the universe – where the divine grace is mediated through the material world. Sam's receptivity to moments of grace, such as the vision of a single star shining through the clouds of Mordor, symbolizes the infusion of hope through faith in God's promise, piercing through the darkness of despair.

In the eschatological perspective, Samwise's journey can be seen as a pilgrimage towards a new creation, a reflection of the Christian's path towards the eschatological hope of heaven. His return to the Shire, armed with the virtues honed through his trials, speaks to the transformative power of hope. It reaffirms the Catholic belief in the potential for renewal and redemption, both personal and communal, through adherence to divine will and trust in God's providential plan.

The figure of Samwise, in his unassuming greatness, serves as a compelling narrative exemplar of the theological virtue of hope. His character provides a profound insight into the power of hope to illuminate the path through the darkest valleys, guiding the faithful towards the ultimate source of light and salvation. In the context of Catholic theology, Samwise embodies the living hope that is central to the Christian faith, a hope that sustains the believer in the journey through this world and beyond.

The lessons drawn from Samwise the Faithful resonate deeply with the Catholic understanding of the human experience, marked by trials, tribulations, and the constant endeavor to remain faithful to God's call. His story, while rooted in the mythic landscape of Middle-Earth, transcends the bounds of fiction to offer timeless truths about the nature of hope, the significance of friendship and loyalty, and the indomitable spirit of the human heart when aligned with divine grace.

In concluding, the apostolate of hope as lived by Samwise the Faithful amplifies the Catholic teachings on the virtues that guide the human soul towards its ultimate end. His narrative is a clarion call to embrace hope, not as an abstract concept, but as a way of life that finds its fulfillment in the love and providence of God. Samwise, in his unwavering commitment and hope, emerges not only as a hero of Middle-Earth but as a spiritual guide for all who journey through the vicissitudes of life, seeking the light of Divine Truth.

Through the lens of Samwise's journey, the Catholic faithful are invited to reflect on the essence of hope as it pertains to their spiritual life and the world around them. In the shadow of Mount Doom, amid despair and destruction, hope prevails, illuminating the path to salvation. Samwise's story, therefore, is not just a tale of Middle-Earth; it is a parable for our times, a testament to the enduring power of hope anchored in faith.

In the grand narrative of faith, hope, and charity, Samwise Gamgee stands as a testament to the quiet strength that lies in hope. As the Apostle of Hope in Tolkien's legendarium, his character serves as a bridge between the world of Middle-Earth and the theological virtues central to Catholic doctrine, offering profound insights into the nature of hope and its pivotal role in the journey of faith.

References:

The Sacramental Reality of Middle-Earth

In traversing from the lush realms of Lothlórien to the shadowed lands of Mordor, the fabric of Middle-Earth is interwoven with symbols and rituals resonating deeply with sacramental reality. The legendarium of J.R.R. Tolkien, while a mythic landscape, mirrors the sacramental ontology that undergirds Catholic thought: the belief that the divine grace is mediated to the material world through sacred signs and rites. Embedded within the narrative of *The Lord of the Rings* are elements that echo the sacramental life, leading the contemplative reader to a deeper understanding of divine mysteries as reflected in the earthly journey.

The provision of Lembas bread to the Fellowship highlights a Eucharistic parallel that can't be overlooked. This elven bread, sustaining the travelers beyond their natural capacity, evokes the sustaining presence of the Eucharist, the Body of Christ, which Catholics believe offers spiritual nourishment and fortifies the soul on its pilgrim journey. Much like the sustenance garnered from the Eucharist, Lembas offers strength and hope in the face of daunting circumstances, embodying the reality of divine assistance in times of great need.

Similarly, Miruvor, the cordial of the elves, serves as a literary analogue to the sacrament of Holy Communion. Consumed in moments of exhaustion and despair, Miruvor revitalizes the spirit and body alike. This mirroring of communion wine, which Catholics hold as the Blood of Christ, signifies the rejuvenation of the heart and soul through divine grace. Through these elements, Tolkien illustrates how the sacred pierces through the profane, offering renewal and strength.

Beyond the sacramental objects within the tale, the very landscape of Middle-Earth speaks to a sacramental understanding of the world. Just as the Catholic faith perceives the whole of creation as a sign pointing towards its Creator, Middle-Earth itself—with its echoing halls of Moria, its verdant fields of the Shire, and its solemn woods of Lothlórien—serves as a testament to the grandeur of something beyond, something sacramentally present. The beauty and terror of the land alike draw its inhabitants to ponder the profound mysteries that lie beyond their comprehension.

One cannot ignore the pivotal role of fellowship in *The Lord of the Rings*. This communal aspect reflects the Church's sacramental life, wherein believers are called into a sacred fellowship. Much like the community of the faithful participating together in the sacraments, the Fellowship of the Ring shares in a united purpose despite their diversity. Their journey mirrors the communal pilgrimage of the Church through the trials of this world, sustained by the sacraments towards the ultimate end of union with the Divine.

Amidst the darkness of Middle-Earth, the light of hope never falters—a hope sustained by the sacramental realities that subtly, yet powerfully, permeate Tolkien's world. This hope aligns with the eschatological dimension of Catholic sacramentology, which points towards the ultimate fulfillment of all creation in the beatific vision. Just as Frodo's journey leads him through the shadow to the ultimate destruction of the Ring, the sacraments guide the soul through the vale of this world towards the light of Eternal Life.

Tolkien's integration of sacramental elements within the narrative framework of Middle-Earth does not serve as mere allegory but rather as a vehicle for illustrating a deeply incarnational view of reality. The material world, in its beauty and brokenness, becomes a means through which divine grace is encountered and through which the reality of redemption is woven into the very fibers of existence. This sacramental vision challenges the reader to see beyond the surface, to find the eternal breaking through the temporal, and to recognize the sacred amidst the ordinary.

In conclusion, the sacramental reality of Middle-Earth holds a mirror to our understanding of the world and our place within it. It beckons us to recognize the myriad ways in which the divine grace seeks us out, sustains us, and draws us towards the fullness of truth. Through his mythic creation, Tolkien extends an invitation to perceive the world eucharistically: as charged with the grandeur of God, wherein every leaf, stone, and drop of water sings of the deeper magic that binds all things.

Lembas Bread: Eucharistic Imagery in The Lord of the Rings

In Tolkien's vast mythopoeic universe, few elements are so infused with sacramental imagery as the elvish waybread, Lembas. This bread, delicate to the touch yet resilient in its sustenance, serves more than a mere narrative function; it is emblematic of the Eucharist in Roman Catholic theology. As Tolkien, a devout Catholic, weaved his story, every thread was imbued with a deeper significance, drawing parallels between his created world and the theological beliefs he held dear.

The essence of Lembas bread is tied to the concept of viaticum, a term in Catholic theology referring to the Eucharist given to a person near death. Though Lembas is provided to the living and hale, its role as sustenance for a perilous journey mirrors the spiritual nourishment intended by the viaticum. The bread given to Frodo and Samwise for their journey into Mordor is not merely food but a sacramental gift that sustains them body and soul. In the darkest of places, it is a beacon of hope and a tangible sign of divine providence.

The preparation of Lembas, cloaked in reverence and mystery, echoes the sacredness surrounding the Eucharist. Just as the Eucharist is consecrated by a priest, the making of Lembas is confined to the Elven maidens, suggesting a ritualistic purity and dedication to its divine purpose. This parallel underscores the profound respect Tolkien had for the sacraments, viewing them as essential intersections between the divine and the mundane.

The effect of Lembas on those who partake of it further aligns with the transformative power attributed to the Eucharist. Recipients describe feeling renewed in spirit, a sentiment that reflects the Catholic understanding of the Eucharist as a source of spiritual strength and grace. This bread, like the body of Christ, offers more than physical sustenance; it provides the strength to endure trials, a theme central to the narrative of The Lord of the Rings.

In the context of Frodo and Sam's journey, Lembas becomes a symbol of unwavering faith. As they traverse the desolate landscape of Mordor, the bread serves as a constant reminder of the light and goodness that still exist in the world. This evokes the concept of memoria, a key aspect of the Catholic Mass where the faithful are called to remember the Last Supper and the sacrifice of Jesus. In Middle-Earth, the sustenance provided by Lembas invokes a remembrance of the Elves and their unwavering fight against the encroaching darkness.

Moreover, the scarcity and sanctity of Lembas amplify its symbolic weight. Only given to those on great quests, it represents the grace that, in Catholic belief, God provides in times of desperate need. This selective provision underscores the theme of divine intervention and the notion that grace is most evident in moments of profound struggle.

The communal aspect of sharing Lembas among the Fellowship mirrors the communal nature of the Eucharist, celebrated during the Mass. It fosters a sense of unity and mutual support, reflecting the Catholic teaching that the Eucharist is a sacrament of communion, binding the faithful together as the Body of Christ.

Furthermore, the reverence with which Lembas is treated by those who carry it speaks to the sacredness imbued within it. Just as the Eucharist is reserved in a tabernacle and approached with solemnity, so too is Lembas wrapped in leaves and kept close, a sacred charge not to be taken lightly. This care and veneration underscore the deeper, sacramental reality that Lembas represents.

Through the lens of Catholic theology, Lembas transcends its role as a mere provision for a journey. It becomes a potent symbol of God's grace, a tangible sign of the divine assistance granted to those embarking on a noble quest. The parallels drawn between Lembas and the Eucharist enrich the narrative, imbuing it with a layer of spiritual depth that resonates with readers long after the final page is turned.

As Tolkien's work invites readers into a deeper contemplation of his story's spiritual dimensions, Lembas stands out as a particularly vivid illustration of the Catholic sacramental imagination. It exemplifies how material elements can be infused with divine grace, elevating the ordinary into a realm of profound spiritual significance.

In conclusion, Lembas bread, in its elvish purity and sustenance, serves as a compelling metaphor for the Eucharist in The Lord of the Rings. It is a testament to the sacramental reality that pervades Middle-Earth, a reminder of the divine presence in all journeys, great and small. As Tolkien's narrative unfolds, the imagery of Lembas bread invites readers to reflect on the presence of grace in their lives, encouraging them to see the sacred in the mundane.

Through the narrative of Frodo and Sam, the sacramental vision of Tolkien reveals the depth of his theological insight, offering a profound meditation on faith, fortitude, and divine providence. Lembas bread, as Eucharistic imagery, becomes a symbol not only of physical sustenance but of spiritual nourishment, guiding the characters – and the readers – through darkness towards the light.

In the woven tapestry of Middle-Earth, Tolkien presents a myriad of elements that find their echoes in the depth of Catholic theology. Among these elements, **Miruvor: The Drink of the Valar and Holy Communion**, stands as an emblematic manifestation of the sacramental reality that permeates Tolkien's universe. This exploration delves into the symbolism and significance of miruvor, comparing and contrasting it with the Holy Communion in the Catholic faith, thereby illuminating its profound theological underpinnings.

Miruvor, known as the cordial of the Valar, is introduced in "The Lord of the Rings" as a reviving drink that offers warmth and renews strength. Its origins are celestial, created by the Valar in Valinor, and its properties are not merely physical but imbue the drinker with a renewed spirit and fortitude. The parallel here with the Eucharist is striking. The Eucharist, central to Catholic worship, is not mere bread and wine but the actual Body and Blood of Christ, offering spiritual nourishment and unity with the divine.

The significance of miruvor extends beyond its immediate effects. It symbolizes the sustenance provided by the divine to aid the faithful in their earthly pilgrimage. Just as the Valar provided miruvor to aid and comfort the inhabitants of Middle-Earth, so does God offer Himself in the Eucharist to accompany and sustain believers through the trials of life. This sacramental understanding emphasizes God's immanence and the tangible means He employs to manifest His grace.

The thematic element of journeying with divine assistance is central to both the narrative of "The Lord of the Rings" and the Christian life. The pilgrim nature of the Fellowship's quest, supported by the sustenance of miruvor, mirrors the Christian pilgrimage towards union with God, fortified by the Eucharist. This parallel illustrates how divine grace is not abstract but participates intimately in the trials and tribulations of the faithful.

Furthermore, the communal aspect of partaking in miruvor among the members of the Fellowship resonates with the communal celebration of the Eucharist. Just as the Fellowship shares miruvor, strengthening their bonds and resolve, so does the Eucharistic celebration unite the body of believers in a profound communion with Christ and with one another. This shared participation manifests the Church's nature as a mystical body and emphasizes the importance of community in the spiritual journey.

The rarity and sacredness of miruvor also parallel the reverence and awe with which the Eucharist is approached in Catholicism. Just as miruvor is reserved for moments of great need and is treated with the utmost respect by those who partake of it, so is the Eucharist celebrated with solemnity and reverence, acknowledging its mystery and the profound grace it bestows.

Moreover, the act of giving miruvor, primarily by Elrond and later by Galadriel, reflects the role of the clergy in administering the sacraments. These characters serve as intermediaries, offering this heavenly gift to aid the journeyers, much like the priests in Catholicism who consecrate and distribute the Eucharist to the faithful.

The transformative power of miruvor, which renews vigor and hope, echoes the transformative grace of the Eucharist, which not only strengthens but also sanctifies the recipient, enabling them to grow in virtue and closer to God. This process of transformation is key to understanding the sacramental reality as a means of becoming who we are called to be in Christ.

However, despite these profound similarities, it's essential to recognize the distinction between the fictional miruvor and the real presence of Christ in the Eucharist. While miruvor serves as a literary symbol that points to a higher reality, the Eucharist is the fulfillment of that reality, the source and summit of the Christian life. This distinction does not diminish the symbolic significance of miruvor but rather highlights the depth of meaning that the Eucharist holds within the Catholic faith.

In conclusion, the exploration of miruvor and its comparison with the Holy Communion offers a rich vein of theological reflection. Tolkien, through his mythopoeic storytelling, presents a sacramental vision of reality where divine grace operates within and through the material world. Miruvor, as the drink of the Valar, serves as a symbol of this sacramental grace, pointing to the ultimate expression of divine love and sustenance in the Eucharist. Thus, within the narrative of Middle-Earth, believers can find echoes of their spiritual journey, illuminated by the sacramental imagination that underlies Tolkien's work.

The contemplation of miruvor and its theological implications invites readers to reflect on the presence of sacramental reality in their lives and the myriad ways in which divine grace manifests. It calls for a deeper appreciation of the Eucharist as the true miruvor, the heavenly food that sustains us on our pilgrimage toward the eternal Valinor.

Marian Figures in Middle-Earth: Galadriel and Beyond

In the textured tapestry of J.R.R. Tolkien's Middle-earth, the echoes of Marian devotion, a cornerstone of Roman Catholic spirituality, can be discerned in the characters and narratives that populate his legendary cosmos. Chief among these echoes is Galadriel, the Lady of Lothlórien, whose portrayal weaves together elements of majesty and mercy, strength and gentleness, in a manner reminiscent of the Virgin Mary. This chapter intends to illuminate these Marian undercurrents, casting light on their implications for a Catholic understanding of creation, providence, and eschatology, within the context of Tolkien's literary oeuvre.

Firstly, Galadriel's role as a source of counsel and comfort to those who journey through her realm mirrors the Marian attribute of mediatrix, one who intercedes on behalf of humanity. This is a quality deeply embedded in Catholic tradition, wherein Mary is considered a compassionate advocate for believers. Galadriel's interaction with the Fellowship, specifically her individual gifts that seem to anticipate their future needs, reflects a foresight and a deep parental care likened to Mary's maternal intercession (Shippey, 2005).

Moreover, Galadriel's act of resisting the temptation of the One Ring evokes the Immaculate Conception, the doctrine that Mary was conceived without original sin. In a world marred by the disfigurement of sin and the shadow of Melkor, Galadriel's purity and her triumphant refusal of the Ring's corrupting power stand as a testament to the possibility of grace in Middle-earth, an echo of Mary's sinlessness and her "yes" to God's will (Flieger, 1997).

The light of Eärendil, contained within the phial given to Frodo, serves not only as a practical aid but as a symbolic representation of hope and spiritual illumination. This light, stemming from a star set in the heavens by the Valar as a sign of divine promise, parallels the star of the Sea, a title for Mary who, in Catholic thought, is seen as a guiding light leading the faithful toward Christ. The phial's role in Frodo's triumph over the darkness of Shelob's lair can be seen as an allegory for Mary's role in the triumph over sin and death (Chance, 2001).

Furthermore, just as Mary plays a pivotal role in Christian eschatology, heralding the ultimate reconciliation between humanity and divinity, Galadriel's departure from Middle-earth signifies an eschatological shift within Tolkien's universe. Her leaving not only marks the end of the Elves' time in Middle-earth but also foretells the rise of Men and the establishment of a new order, aligning with the Catholic vision of history's purposeful progression towards a divine culmination.

Yet, Galadriel is not the sole Marian figure in Tolkien's work. Characters such as Éowyn and Rosie Cotton, though less overtly imbued with Marian symbolism, embody virtues commonly associated with Mary, such as courage, purity, and a nurturing spirit. These characters enrich Tolkien's narrative, creating a multifaceted Marian presence that intertwines with the story's themes of sacrifice, redemption, and hope.

In analyzing these characters and themes, it becomes evident that Tolkien's Catholic imagination pervades his depiction of female characters, embedding within them qualities that reflect his ecclesiastical reverence for Mary. It is through these characters that Tolkien explores and celebrates aspects of Marian dogma — her divine maternity, immaculate nature, and role in salvation history — albeit in a sub-creational context.

These Marian figures serve as beacons of light and sources of hope, guiding characters toward their destiny and embodying the virtues necessary to confront and overcome the darkness. Through their actions, commitment, and faith, these figures illuminate the path of providence, revealing the workings of grace in the world of Middle-earth. This reflects the Catholic conviction of divine providence — the belief in a benevolent, omnipotent, and omniscient God who guides creation towards its eschatological fulfillment.

In conclusion, the exploration of Marian figures in Middle-earth, particularly through the lens of Galadriel, unveils Tolkien's profound integration of his faith into the fabric of his literary creation. By weaving together themes of grace, redemption, and divine maternity, Tolkien articulates a vision of the world imbued with theological depth and spiritual resonance, inviting readers to perceive the glimmerings of divine truth through the veil of myth.

The Marian figures of Middle-earth, in their complexity and diversity, stand as a testament to Tolkien's ability to transcend the boundaries of genre, crafting a narrative that not only entertains but enlightens, beckoning toward the deeper mysteries of faith, hope, and love that lie at the heart of Catholic doctrine.

The Virtue of Humility: Lessons from Hobbits and Heroes

The tapestry of Middle-Earth, woven with threads of courage, valor, and sacrifice, also highlights the equally significant yet often overlooked virtue of humility. Within the realm of Tolkien's creation, instances of humility shed light on the characters' underlying strength, revealing how this virtue serves as a cornerstone in their moral and spiritual development. Particularly, the roles of hobbits and key figures like Galadriel exemplify the profound power and beauty of humility in a world teetering on the brink of darkness.

The essence of hobbits, with their simple ways and love for the quiet life, stands in stark contrast to the grandeur and might often celebrated in tales of heroism. Yet, it is their humility that ultimately heralds their greatness. The small, unassuming hobbits demonstrate that true humility does not mean thinking less of oneself, but thinking of oneself less, focusing on the greater good beyond personal glory. This lesson is vividly illustrated in Frodo's willingness to bear the Ring, fully aware of his limitations and the monumental scale of his task.

Galadriel, the Lady of Lothlórien, presents another fascinating study of humility. Despite her immense power and wisdom, Galadriel's greatest moment comes when she rejects the Ring of Power. In acknowledging her potential for corruption, her act of refusal mirrors the humility inherent in recognizing one's vulnerabilities and the strength found in restraint. This moment not only underscores the Marian parallel of humility as purity and strength but also aligns with the Catholic understanding that true humility lies in the acknowledgment of one's dependence on the Divine.

In the humble actions of both hobbits and heroes, one observes a reflection of divine humility. The concept, deeply entrenched in Catholic theology, posits God's willingness to become man, embracing suffering and death, as the ultimate act of humility. This theological cornerstone resonates within Tolkien's creation, where the mightiest are often those who serve and sacrifice, thereby echoing the servant leadership exemplified by Christ.

The encounter between Galadriel and Frodo serves as a pivotal moment where humility is explored in depth. Galadriel, faced with her deepest temptation, and Frodo, burdened by an almost insurmountable task, both reveal their greatness through their humble acceptance of their roles in the unfolding divine plan. This parallel draws attention to the significance of humility in the journey of faith, symbolizing the relinquishment of one's will to the divine providence.

The narrative arc of Samwise Gamgee further exemplifies humility's virtue. His unwavering loyalty and service, devoid of any aspiration for recognition, highlight how humility fosters genuine relationships and collaborations. Sam's humility, characterized by his self-giving love, stands as a testament to the power of simple acts of kindness and steadfastness in the face of adversity.

The humility displayed by hobbits and key figures like Galadriel and Gandalf, who acknowledges his limitations despite his power, serves as a beacon of hope. It is a powerful reminder that, in the grand tapestry of life, the smallest threads can hold together the most significant patterns. The humility of these characters does not diminish their strength but rather fortifies it, offering profound lessons in leadership, service, and the essence of true heroism.

Through their narratives, Tolkien illuminates humility not as a sign of weakness but as a reservoir of strength. It is through their humility that characters like Frodo and Aragorn achieve their destined greatness, not by relying on their own might, but by placing their trust in something greater than themselves. This perspective aligns with the Catholic view that humanity's strength lies in recognizing its limitations and dependence on God's will.

The portrayal of humility in Middle-Earth also serves as a critique of the pride and hubris that lead to downfall—a recurring theme in Tolkien's works. Characters who exhibit excessive pride, such as Saruman and Denethor, contrast sharply with the humble heroes, underscoring the destructive nature of pride and the salvific quality of humility.

Hobbits, embodying the everyman, bring the virtue of humility closer to the reader's world, suggesting that heroism lies within reach of those who choose selflessness over self-aggrandizement. Their journey from the Shire to the very heart of darkness and back again is a testament to the strength found in humility, endurance, and the courage to do what is right, regardless of the odds.

In the broader theological context, Tolkien's narrative harmonizes with the Catholic understanding that humility serves as the foundation for a virtuous life. It echoes the Beatitudes, where the meek and the peacemakers are blessed, highlighting the paradoxical strength found in humility and the promise of redemption it holds.

The virtue of humility, as depicted through hobbits and heroes in Middle-Earth, offers a profound spiritual lesson. It teaches that greatness often comes not from dominion or strength but from the quiet, steadfast heart willing to serve, sacrifice, and place trust in the providence of a guidance greater than oneself.

Thus, "The Virtue of Humility: Lessons from Hobbits and Heroes" delves into the heart of Tolkien's Middle-Earth, revealing that the most enduring power—capable of confronting the greatest darkness—is found not in towering fortresses or in the hands of mighty warriors, but in the quiet, humble hearts of those who choose to serve something beyond themselves.

Ultimately, the humility presented in Tolkien's universe invites reflection on our own lives. It encourages us to consider how humility might not only shape our personal narratives but also affect the world. By embracing our limitations and placing our trust in a higher power, we, too, can embark on a path filled with purpose, hope, and unforeseen greatness, mirrored in the humble footsteps of hobbits and the wise restraint of heroes.

Aragorn: The King as Servant and Priest In the vast tapestry of Middle-Earth, few characters embody the integration of royal authority and humble service as completely as Aragorn son of Arathorn. Through the lens of Catholic theology, Aragorn's life and mission echo the Paschal mystery of Christ, serving as an exemplar of the king who is at once a servant and a priest. This chapter seeks to unveil the depth of Aragorn's character as a confluence of kingly majesty and priestly humility, illustrating how these qualities illuminate the Catholic understanding of leadership and sacrifice.

In J.R.R. Tolkien's narrative, Aragorn's journey from Strider, the Ranger of the North, to King Elessar of the Reunited Kingdom represents a path of selfless dedication to the good of Middle-Earth. His initial anonymity and humble guise as a wanderer mask the royal bloodline and the potential for greatness that lies within him. This motif of hidden kingship resonates with the Christocentric principle of kenosis, the self-emptying of one's own will to embrace God's will, which is central to Catholic soteriology.

The very nature of Aragorn's claim to the throne is built upon an act of service; he does not seek power for its own sake but understands his royal heritage as a call to serve the peoples of Middle-Earth. His eventual ascent to the throne is contingent upon his willingness to lay down his life for his friends and subjects, mirroring the ultimate sacrifice Christ made on the cross. Aragorn's journey, fraught with peril and sacrifice, culminates in the restoration of the kingdom, a task he could achieve only by embracing his role as a servant-leader.

Aragorn's assumption of the kingship further reveals his priestly role within the narrative. As king, he becomes a mediator between the past and present, the living and the dead, embodying the priestly function of intercession. His healing hands, which bring relief and restoration to Faramir, Éowyn, and Merry, among others, signify the messianic prophecy of Isaiah, recalling the priestly role of Christ as healer and redeemer.

This healing ministry underscores the sacramental imagination of Middle-Earth, wherein physical actions carry spiritual significance. The hands of the king, which evoke both reverence and awe, become instruments of divine grace, echoing the Catholic understanding of sacraments as visible signs of invisible grace. Aragorn, in his capacity to heal, acts as a conduit of divine benediction, revealing the interplay between his kingly authority and priestly service.

Moreover, Aragorn's leadership is deeply Eucharistic, embodying the principle of self-gift. His willingness to walk the Paths of the Dead, risking all for the sake of his people, parallels the Eucharistic sacrifice, where Christ offers himself for the life of the world. It is through this ultimate act of courage and self-sacrifice that Aragorn secures the allegiance of the Dead Men of Dunharrow, a moment that highlights the salvific power of self-offering.

Aragorn's marriage to Arwen also serves as a sacramental sign, reflecting the nuptial imagery prevalent in the Bible to describe Christ's relationship with the Church. This union not only signifies the harmonious restoration of two long-sundered kindreds but also represents the eschatological hope of the New Jerusalem, where Christ, the Lamb, is united with his Bride, the Church.

It's also noteworthy that Aragorn's governance as king embodies the virtues of prudence, justice, fortitude, and temperance — the cardinal virtues in Catholic moral teaching. His rule ushers in an era of peace and prosperity, reflecting the scriptural promise of the peaceable kingdom where the lion lies down with the lamb. His reign, marked by wisdom and compassion, embodies the ideal of the servant-king, who governs not by dominion, but by virtue.

Lastly, Aragorn's departure to the Undying Lands, reminiscent of a peaceful death that is more akin to a transition than an end, encapsulates the Catholic hope of eternal life. In his leaving, he embodies the Christian belief in the resurrection and the life everlasting, offering a model of faithful living and dying that resonates deeply with the Catholic eschatological vision.

Through the character of Aragorn, Tolkien crafts a multifaceted portrait of kingship that integrates the roles of servant and priest. This confluence of royal and sacerdotal imagery not only enriches the narrative of The Lord of the Rings but also offers profound insights into the nature of leadership, service, and sacrifice from a Catholic perspective.

By examining Aragorn's life and mission through the prism of Catholic theology, one discerns the silhouette of Christ in the figure of the king — a ruler whose strength lies not in the exercise of power but in the power of self-giving love. In this regard, Aragorn emerges as an archetype of the Christian leader, whose kingship and priesthood illuminate the path to true greatness, marked by humility, service, and sacrifice.

In conclusion, the character of Aragorn serves as a beacon of hope, symbolizing the reconciliation of all things in Christ. Through his dual role as king and priest, Aragorn embodies the Catholic vision of redemptive leadership, where authority is exercised as a form of service, and sacrifice is seen as the pathway to restoration and peace. His story, interwoven with themes of providence, redemption, and eternal life, invites readers to reflect on the Christian call to servanthood, priesthood, and ultimately, sainthood.

The Power of Prayer and Providence in Middle-Earth

In the grand tapestry of Tolkien's Middle-Earth, the threads of prayer and providence are interwoven with such subtlety and depth that its study reveals a complex theological underpinning reminiscent of the most profound Roman Catholic teachings. This chapter aims to unveil how these elements not only shape the narrative but also reflect upon the nature of divinity, free will, and destiny in Tolkien's universe. While Middle-Earth is a fictional realm, its spiritual and moral compass points toward very real and central Catholic doctrines of creation, providence, and the ultimate good overcoming evil through divine intervention and mortal cooperation.

The epic saga unfolding across Middle-Earth can be viewed as a journey through darkness towards enlightenment, guided by the silent whispers of providence. The concept of providence, or divine foreknowledge and care, is pivotal in understanding Tolkien's portrayal of the struggle between good and evil. In the fabric of Middle-Earth, every thread - no matter how insignificant it seems - is part of a larger design orchestrated by Eru Ilúvatar, the supreme deity. This divine design does not infringe upon the free will granted to Ilúvatar's creations. Instead, it represents a harmonious balance between divine omnipotence and creaturely freedom (Shippey, 2003).

Prayer in Middle-Earth, though not overtly ritualistic, is profoundly spiritual, reflective of a deep-seated trust in a higher power's guiding hand. Instances of prayer in Tolkien's narratives often occur in moments of despair, illustrating a turning towards faith when faced with insurmountable odds. These moments, though subtle, underscore a reliance on divine assistance and an acknowledgment of the interconnectedness of all beings within Ilúvatar's creation.

The Fellowship's journey is emblematic of the Catholic understanding of pilgrimage - a physical journey mirroring a spiritual quest towards divine grace. Here, Tolkien masterfully illustrates how providence works through ordinary individuals performing extraordinary acts. Frodo's acceptance of the burden of the Ring, akin to a form of prayerful submission, sets into motion a series of events underpinned by providential care.

In discussing the paradox of Middle-Earth's destiny, one must acknowledge that Tolkien's world embraces the Catholic doctrine of dual predestination lightly, hinting at an ultimate destination guided by benevolence. Divine foreknowledge in Middle-Earth does not preclude the exercise of free will; instead, it coexists, allowing for the unfolding of history as a collaborative creation between the Divine and its subjects (Wood, 2003).

The problem of evil, approached through the lens of Ilúvatar's plan, becomes a profound meditation on the necessity of suffering and the power of redemption. Melkor's discord in the Music of the Ainur introduces disharmony, yet it is through this very strife that the greatest acts of heroism, sacrifice, and love emerge. This interplay highlights the Catholic belief in God's ability to bring about a greater good from evil, affirming the omnipotence and omnibenevolence of the divine (Caldecott, 2012).

Furthermore, the role of the Valar and the Maiar illuminates the Catholic understanding of angelic beings as intermediaries of God's will. Gandalf, a Maia, serves as a guardian and guide, his interventions often reflecting divine providence. His resurrection and return as Gandalf the White underscore the theme of death and rebirth, resonant with the Catholic significance of resurrection as a symbol of hope and redemption.

Amidst these cosmic battles and epic journeys, the most profound demonstrations of prayer and providence occur in the smallest of actions: Sam's unwavering loyalty to Frodo, Bilbo's pity towards Gollum, and the Ents' decision to march against Isengard. These acts, fueled by virtues of faith, hope, and charity, embody the power of prayer without words. They reveal the profound truth that in Middle-Earth, as in the Catholic faith, divine grace works through the willing heart, transforming the mundane into the miraculous.

In conclusion, the power of prayer and providence in Middle-Earth serves not only as a narrative device but as a theological reflection on the Roman Catholic understanding of the divine. Tolkien's legendarium, rich with symbolism and allegory, invites a contemplative engagement with the mysteries of faith, free will, and divine justice. It beckons the reader to recognize the presence of a guiding hand in the unfolding of the world's history and in the intricacies of their own lives.

As Catholic theology teaches, God's providence is a tapestry of love, woven with the threads of human freedom and divine will. Middle-Earth, in all its mythical splendor, mirrors this profound truth, revealing the silent workings of the divine in the lives of its inhabitants. Thus, in exploring the realms of Middle-Earth, one embarks on a journey of faith, discovering the quiet yet omnipotent force of prayer and providence guiding the destiny of all creation.

The exploration of prayer and providence in Middle-Earth, though grounded in Catholic doctrine, transcends religious boundaries, offering insights into the universal quest for understanding the divine's role in the world's suffering and triumphs. Tolkien's narrative becomes a beacon of hope, affirming the triumph of good over evil, light over darkness, and the ultimate victory of divine providence in the tapestry of creation.

References:

Caldecott, S. (2012). The Power of the Ring: The Spiritual Vision Behind The Lord of the Rings. Crossroad Publishing.

Shippey, T. (2003). J.R.R. Tolkien: Author of the Century. HarperCollins.

Wood, R. (2003). The Gospel According to Tolkien: Visions of the Kingdom in Middle-earth. Westminster John Knox Press.

Divine Foreknowledge and Free Will: The Paradox of Middle-Earth's Destiny

In the tapestry of Middle-Earth's history, as woven by Tolkien, the threads of free will and divine foreknowledge intertwine in a complex pattern that challenges and engages both theology and philosophy. At the heart of this interplay lies the enigmatic nature of Eru Ilúvatar, whose omniscience does not negate the autonomy of the Arda's inhabitants. This paradox, one that echoes deeply within Roman Catholic thought, invites an exploration of how divine providence coexists with the freedom granted to all beings in Middle-Earth.

The unfolding narrative of Middle-Earth, especially as it pertains to the events leading to the downfall of Sauron, serves as a profound exploration of the workings of providence amidst the choices of free beings. Despite Eru's omnipotent foresight, the characters within Tolkien's universe navigate their paths, making decisions that stem from their own wills. This dynamic elucidates a fundamental tenet of Catholic teaching on free will and divine knowledge: that God's foreknowledge of future events does not compel these events to occur (Aquinas, Summa Theologica, I, q. 14, a. 13).

The pivotal moment in "The Lord of the Rings," where Frodo freely chooses to claim the Ring for himself, yet the Ring is destroyed regardless, underscores this theme. This event might seem, at first glance, to suggest a determinism, where the end was fixed despite the choices made. However, a deeper contemplation reveals that it was the freely made choices of numerous characters, influenced by grace yet not determined by it, that led to this climax. Here, Tolkien showcases that while Eru's plan encompasses the end, it is through the freely made choices of the individuals that the purpose is fulfilled.

Another illuminating aspect is observed in the journey of Aragorn. His path to kingship, foretold by prophecy, could be misconstrued as a predestined course void of free will. Yet, it was through his decisions, courage, and ultimately, his acceptance of his role, that the prophecy was fulfilled. This echoes the Catholic understanding of prophecy as not just foretelling the future but inviting participation in bringing about that future through free responses to God's grace.

The mystery of providence and free will is further explored through the actions of characters who seemingly act against Eru's design, such as Boromir's attempt to take the Ring. These actions, while autonomous, are nonetheless woven into the larger narrative Eru has in mind, showcasing the divine ability to incorporate even the wayward choices of free beings into a greater good (Catechism of the Catholic Church, 1994, §311-312).

The role of prayer in Middle-Earth acts as a conduit between the will of the individual and the divine will, suggesting a collaborative process rather than a unilateral imposition of fate. When Frodo prays in the depths of Mount Doom, it is an act of free will seeking divine assistance, not a surrender to an inevitable destiny. This reflects the Catholic understanding of prayer as a means of aligning one's will with God's, participating freely in the unfolding of divine providence (Catechism of the Catholic Church, 1994, §2559-2565).

The concept of 'eucatastrophe,' a term coined by Tolkien himself, serves as a narrative reflection of this theological paradox. The unforeseen good turn at the story's climax—a direct intervention of grace—does not negate the free actions of the characters but instead brings them to fruition in a way that reveals the overarching plan of good overcoming evil.

The intricate relationship between divine foreknowledge and free will in Middle-Earth opens a window into the Catholic understanding of these concepts. It reveals a cosmos where divine omnipotence and omniscience harmoniously coexist with the free will of created beings—a universe where the ultimate victory of good is assured, not by the annulment of free will, but through its sanctification and fulfillment in the embrace of divine providence.

Thus, the paradox of Middle-Earth's destiny serves as a profound allegory for the dynamic interplay of free will and divine foreknowledge within the Catholic faith. Tolkien's narrative artistry invites believers to ponder the mysteries of their faith, seeing in the struggles and triumphs of Middle-Earth a mirror of their own journey towards the fulfillment of divine providence.

In examining these themes through the lens of Tolkien's mythology, readers are invited to reflect on the profound compatibility between human freedom and divine omniscience. The characters of Middle-Earth, in their freely made decisions, carry out the divine plan laid out by Eru, embodying the Catholic belief that divine providence does not infringe upon but rather uplifts and completes the exercise of free will.

Therefore, the narrative of Middle-Earth does not merely entertain; it serves as a theological and philosophical meditation on the profound truths of existence, destiny, and the divine. It reassures the faithful that their choices matter, that free will is a precious gift, and that divine providence is always at work, guiding the universe towards its ultimate good.

In conclusion, the paradox of Middle-Earth's destiny, as explored through the rich tapestry of Tolkien's creation, offers a profound reflection on the mysteries of divine foreknowledge and human freedom. It challenges the faithful to contemplate the depth of God's plan, recognizing that within the bounds of divine providence, there lies the liberating truth that free will is not only preserved but is integral to the fulfillment of that divine plan. In this reflection, Tolkien's mythopoetic universe shines as a beacon of theological and philosophical inquiry, inviting an ever-deeper exploration of the mysteries of faith.

The Problem of Evil: Understanding Ilúvatar's Plan The contemplation of Eru Ilúvatar's plan amidst the resounding echoes of discord and the palpable presence of evil in Middle-Earth demands a nuanced understanding. Within this realm, forged by the primordial music, every note of discord seemingly challenges the precept of a benevolent creator. This conundrum, deeply rooted in Catholic theology as well, stirs the intellect and kindles the soul's search for meaning beyond the audial tumult of the world.

The world that Ilúvatar envisioned, and the Ainur helped to shape, was not without its flaws from inception, much like the world we inhabit. The entry of Melkor's cacophony into the Music of the Ainur introduces a thematic element that resonates through the ages: that of a creation marred by the rebellion of a part of the creation itself. From such a standpoint, the presence of evil in Middle-Earth is not a mere happenstance but a fundamental part of its very fabric, much as it is in our understanding of the Catholic faith.

In the shadows of this discord, the question arises: Why would a benevolent Ilúvatar permit such dissonance? The answer lies tangled in the melodies of free will and divine purpose. Ilúvatar, in His omnipotence, permits the Ainur, and subsequently the inhabitants of Middle-Earth, the autonomy to choose, to err, and to stray. Yet, within such freedom lies the immense potential for redemption, for turning back to the harmony intended by Ilúvatar.

The narrative of Middle-Earth, thus, transcends a mere battle between good and evil; it unfolds as a testament to Ilúvatar's faith in His creation. The struggles that pervade this world are not signs of Ilúvatar's absence but evidences of His subtle governance, directing all towards an ultimate eucatastrophe. The Catholic faith mirrors this belief in a providential God who permits evil only to bring forth a greater good, a theme deeply entrenched in Tolkien's writings.

Amidst the darkness wrought by Melkor and his minions, the light of Ilúvatar's children gleams with an undiminished resolve. Their valor, love, and sacrifice illuminate the darkest corridors of Middle-Earth, reinforcing the belief in a greater plan. These acts of goodness, often emerging from the most humble of sources, underscore a profound Catholic conviction: Each soul possesses an innate capacity to reflect divine light, regardless of the encompassing darkness.

Furthermore, the role of suffering within Middle-Earth offers a reflection of Catholic teachings on redemptive suffering. The travails encountered by the denizens of this world serve not as mere trials but as pathways to elevate their spirits, drawing them closer to the ultimate harmony envisioned by Ilúvatar. It is in accepting and transcending suffering that characters such as Frodo, Aragorn, and even Gollum find their true essence and purpose.

The presence of evil and the resultant suffering thereby lead not to despair but to a deepened understanding and an enriched faith in Ilúvatar's grand orchestration. The Catholic ethos, seeing value in suffering, finds a parallel in Tolkien's universe where each setback is a step towards a greater awakening, each loss a gain in the grand tally of the cosmos.

In confronting the problem of evil, it is imperative to recognize the role of human (and elvish) agency. The atrocities committed by Sauron and his followers stem from a misuse of the gift of free will, a theme resonant with the Catholic understanding of sin. Yet, within this capacity for wrongdoing lies the equally potent capability for redemption, for turning towards the light, a dynamic vividly captured through the arcs of characters like Boromir and Théoden.

Ilúvatar's ultimate plan, therefore, emerges not despite the presence of evil, but through it. The discord woven into the Music of the Ainur finds resolution in the unforeseen harmonies it engenders—harmonies born of choice, sacrifice, and a steadfast belief in the underlying goodness of Ilúvatar's creation. This intrinsic hope, this belief in the eventual triumph of good, mirrors the Catholic understanding of salvation history, where evil, though momentary, necessitates the unfolding of divine providence.

The eucatastrophe, a term coined by Tolkien, encapsulates this interplay between despair and hope, between discord and harmony. The sudden and unexpected turns for the better, signifying Ilúvatar's handiwork, underlie the narrative's most pivotal moments. These instances of grace highlight the omnipresence of Ilúvatar, ensuring that no evil is so great that good cannot emerge from it.

Thus, the problem of evil in Middle-Earth, much like in our own world, cannot be understood in isolation. It serves as a backdrop against which the brilliance of Ilúvatar's creation reveals itself. Evil, in its essence, becomes a tool, albeit a painful one, in sculpting the souls of Middle-Earth towards their ultimate destiny—a destiny intertwined with Ilúvatar's unfathomable plan.

In essence, the narrative of Middle-Earth unfolds as a grand theological symposium, dialoguing with the deepest quandaries of the human soul. The presence of evil, rather than negating the existence of a benevolent Ilúvatar, accentuates His omnipotence, wisdom, and, above all, His boundless love for creation. It is through the very trials and tribulations born of evil that the inhabitants of Middle-Earth, and by extension, we ourselves, are drawn into an ever-closer communion with the divine.

In this light, Tolkien's creation serves not merely as an escape but as a mirror, reflecting our struggles, fears, and hopes. It invites us to see beyond the immediate turmoil and to trust in the ever-unfurling plan of Ilúvatar—a plan that encompasses, transforms, and transcends the problem of evil, guiding all towards an ultimate reunion in the undying lands.

The profound intermingling of free will, divine providence, and the presence of evil in Tolkien's universe offers a rich tapestry for contemplation. It allows us to explore the depths of faith, the nature of God, and our place within His creation, enriching our understanding and appreciation of both Tolien's work and the Catholic doctrine.

The Journey Beyond: Death and the Afterlife in Tolkien's World

In the realm of Middle-Earth, the concept of death and the afterlife holds a unique place that mirrors, yet distinctively diverges from, traditional Roman Catholic doctrine. As we delve into the intricate world crafted by J.R.R. Tolkien, it becomes evident that his portrayal of the journey beyond life is not only a central theme in his legendarium but also a profound commentary on the nature of fate, immortality, and the soul's longing for eternity.

The fate of Elves and Men in Tolkien's universe presents a fascinating study of contrast and similarity to Catholic teachings on the afterlife. Elves, blessed with immortality, are bound to the world until its end, while Men possess the 'Gift of Men,' a term used by Tolkien to signify mortality and the destiny of humans to leave the world and go beyond— a concept enveloped in mystery, akin to the Christian understanding of eternal life beyond the temporal realm (Shippey, 2000).

For Elves, death is seen as an unnatural state, a sundering of the fëa and hröa—spirit and body—whereas Men view it as an inherent aspect of their existence, a passage into a realm beyond Arda where Eru Ilúvatar awaits. This dichotomy raises intriguing theological discussions concerning the Catholic perspective on death and immortality, drawing parallels and discerning the differences in how each fate is perceived as part of Eru's divine plan.

The tragic tale of the Númenóreans, particularly their desire for immortality and the cataclysmic consequences of their rebellion against their mortal fate, serves as a poignant critique of humanity's yearning for what lies beyond their grasp. In a manner that mirrors the biblical narrative of the Tower of Babel, their downfall underscores a significant moral lesson within both Catholic theology and Tolkien's narrative: the peril inherent in striving to transcend divinely ordained limits (Flieger, 2002).

Conversely, the journey of Frodo Baggins encapsulates the Catholic virtue of hope amidst despair. His passage through death's shadow and the ultimate healing at the Undying Lands can be seen as an allegory for the Christian promise of salvation and eternal peace. It reflects a pivotal Catholic teaching on the redemptive value of suffering and the hope of resurrection, reinforcing the eschatological vision that Tolkien subtly wove into the fabric of his fantasy.

The resilience of Samwise Gamgee further exemplifies the notion of eschatological hope. His unwavering faith and loyalty, characteristics that resonate with the cardinal virtues of the

Catholic tradition, illuminate the pathway through darkness towards a promised future. Sam's return to the Shire, though marred by the scars of his journey, symbolizes the Christian's journey through life's trials towards the promise of eternal bliss.

Moreover, Tolkien's depiction of the Halls of Mandos, where the spirits of Elves (and some select others) await their fate, serves as a meditation on the Catholic concept of purgatory. It is a place not of punishment, but of waiting and potential purification, offering a parallel to the Catholic understanding of a transitional state where souls are prepared for their final communion with the Divine (Hammond & Scull, 2005).

The enigmatic 'Doors of Night,' through which the spirits of Men depart from the world, resonate with the Christian mystery of death. This threshold, which even the Valar cannot see beyond, signifies the leap of faith at the heart of both Tolkien's mythology and Catholic eschatology. The Doors underscore the ultimate hope and trust in a benevolent Creator who guides the destiny of all creation.

The role of memory and legacy in the face of mortality also provides a rich field for theological reflection. The Elves, in their immortal longings and sorrow over the passing of time, capture the human desire to transcend the temporal, to leave a mark that endures. This notion echoes the Catholic emphasis on the communion of saints, the spiritual solidarity between the living and the dead, and the lasting impact of one's life on the world.

Finally, Tolkien's sub-creation offers a sacramental view of reality, one where material creation participates in and signifies a higher reality. Death and the afterlife in Tolkien's work can thus be seen as a sacrament in narrative form: an outward sign of an inward grace, pointing to realities beyond human comprehension but firmly rooted in divine promise.

In conclusion, exploring death and the afterlife in Tolkien's world reveals a tapestry of themes that resonate deeply with Catholic doctrine, yet are portrayed in a way that is both unique to Tolkien's mythopoeic vision and accessible to a wider audience. Through his fantasy, Tolkien invites us on a journey of faith, hope, and reflection on our own mortality and the promise of eternal life, challenging us to see beyond the veil of this world to the eternal truths that lie beyond.

The Fate of Elves and Men: Examining The Tolkienian Afterlife

In the expansive mythology of Middle-Earth crafted by J.R.R. Tolkien, the journey beyond death for Elves and Men forms a cornerstone of the narrative's theological and philosophical framework. The delineation of their destinies not only enriches the narrative texture but also provides a conduit for examining broader ontological themes within Tolkien's world. This section aims to scrutinize the fate of these two races in the afterlife, delving into the nuances of their respective immortality and mortality as well as the implications of these conditions within a Catholic theological perspective.

Elves, as depicted by Tolkien, are bound to the world for its duration. Their spirits, upon death, travel to the Halls of Mandos in Valinor, where they may rest, reflect, and, in some cases, be reincarnated back into the world. This cycle embodies a form of immortality that is distinctively their "gift," but it is also a source of their profound melancholia. The Elves' eternal tie to the world's fate ensures their joy and sorrow are inexorably linked to its fortunes. This concept can be pondered through the lens of Catholic doctrine, which speaks to the innate longing for the eternal present in every created being. Unlike Elves, Men in Tolkien's legendarium are not bound to the world; they possess the 'Gift of Men,' which is the freedom to depart from the world entirely upon death, a concept shrouded in mystery and hope.

Men's departure to unknown fates beyond the Circles of the World sparks a discussion surrounding human destiny and the Catholic doctrine of the afterlife. It reflects an inherent hope, a theological virtue that Catholic tradition holds dear. The ambiguity surrounding the destination of Men's spirits after death suggests an anticipation of a transcendent fulfillment, reminiscent of the Christian hope in the resurrection and life everlasting. This resonates with the Catholic understanding of human mortality, where death opens the door to a new communion with the Divine, beyond the margins of the physical world.

The Elves' perception of Men's mortality often as enviable underscores a profound theological insight: that mortality, wrapped in the Catholic notion of a hopeful passage towards God, can indeed be seen as a 'gift' in its own right. It is a liberation from the temporal, a journey towards an ultimate union with the Divine, which the Elf-legendarium only vaguely grasitates towards. This viewpoint aligns with Catholic eschatology which views death not as an end but as a threshold to eternal life.

However, departing from the Catholic conception of the afterlife as a communal experience in the presence of God, Tolkien's Elves face a unique form of solitariness in their fate. Their eternal bond to the Earthly realm, while granting them a measure of immortality, also isolates them from the transcendental destiny that awaits Men. This contrast illuminates a crucial aspect of Tolkien's theology: the exploration of isolation and communion as states of being in the afterlife.

The narrative also delves into the concept of freewill and its implications for the afterlife destinies of both races. Elves and Men make pivotal choices that shape their paths in the world and beyond. In this context, Catholic doctrine emphasizes the significance of freewill in the moral and spiritual development of souls, positioning life as a journey towards or away from the divine essence. Tolkien mirrors this sentiment, showcasing how choices anchored in virtue or vice can alter destinies.

The destiny of Men in Tolkien's universe, having the Gift of Mortality, raises poignant questions about the nature of freedom and the ultimate desire for unification with the transcendent. It touches upon the Catholic understanding of death as a passage, a movement towards consummation with the divine, a theme that Tolkien subtly weaves into the tapestry of his narrative through the mortal journey of Men.

Another intriguing aspect to consider is the role of memory and legacy in the Elves' immortality. Their eternal lives are deeply intertwined with the history of Middle-Earth, making them living witnesses to the unfolding of ages. In contrast, Men's legacies are preserved in their deeds, stories, and the continuation of their lineages, reflecting a Catholic appreciation for the sacredness of history and tradition as vessels of divine action in the world.

In conclusion, the fate of Elves and Men in Tolkien's cosmos offers a rich tapestry for exploring theological and philosophical concepts central to Catholic doctrine. The contrasting destinies of these races illuminate themes of immortality, mortality, hope, and the journey of the soul beyond death. Tolkien constructs a mythopoetic universe wherein the fate of its inhabitants echoes the complexities of human spiritual longing and the quest for ultimate truth.

Examining the Tolkienian afterlife through a Catholic lens reveals the depth and breadth of Tolkien's theological imagination, inviting readers to reflect on the mysteries of life, death, and what lies beyond. It presents a narrative world where the fate of its characters not only entertains but also enlightens, offering glimpses into the profound theological truths that underpin the human condition.

References:

Flieger, V. (2002). Splintered Light: Logos and Language in Tolkien's World. Kent State University Press.

Shippey, T. (2000). J.R.R. Tolkien: Author of the Century. Houghton Mifflin.

Tolkien, J.R.R. (1954). The Lord of the Rings. George Allen & Unwin.

Númenórean Desires for Immortality: A Catholic Critique

In the mythic tapestry of J.R.R. Tolkien's legendarium, the tale of Númenor stands as a poignant exploration of the theme of mortality and the desire for immortality. At the heart of this narrative is a critique deeply resonant with Catholic theology, offering a profound reflection on the human condition, the longing for eternal life, and the pitfalls of attempting to overstep divinely ordained limits. The tragic downfall of Númenor serves as a cautionary tale that navigates through the complex interplay of free will, divine providence, and the natural order established by Eru Ilúvatar.

According to the lore, the men of Númenor were blessed with long life, yet they fell into despair and rebellion against the ban of the Valar, which prohibited them from sailing westward to the Undying Lands, a place of immortality reserved for the Elves. Their growing obsession with the fear of death and the desire for eternal life echoes the Catholic understanding of concupiscence: the human inclination towards sin, marked by a disordered desire for earthly pleasures. In Catholic theology, while the natural desire for eternal happiness is inscribed in the human heart, seeking it outside of God's will leads to spiritual ruin (Catechism of the Catholic Church, 1997).

The story of Númenor is not merely a fantastical narrative but parallels the biblical tale of the Tower of Babel. Both stories depict humanity's hubris in attempting to attain divine status or dwellings by their means, disregarding divine commandments. This theme is emblematically Catholic, reflecting the teaching that pride is the root of all sin, and it is in humility and obedience to divine will that true greatness is found.

From a Catholic viewpoint, the downfall of Númenor also illustrates the doctrine of original sin and its consequences. Just as Adam and Eve were exiled from Eden for their disobedience, so too were the Númenóreans driven to ruin for their rebellion against the divine ban. However, Tolkien's narrative, consistent with Catholic eschatology, retains a thread of hope: the 'faithful' remnant of Númenor, who remained loyal to Eru and the Valar, were spared and led to a new land. This echoes the promise of salvation and the possibility of redemption through faith and fidelity to divine laws.

The longing for immortality expressed by the Númenóreans reflects a profound theological truth acknowledged in Catholicism: the human soul's inherent desire for eternal life with God. However, the path to this eternal life deviates significantly between the Númenórean approach and Catholic teaching. Where the Númenóreans sought to grasp immortality through their power and defiance, Catholicism calls for surrender to God's will and grace as the means to attain eternal life.

The Church teaches that true immortality and fulfillment are found not in this world but in the beatific vision of God in the next (Catechism of the Catholic Church, 2000). This teaching highlights a critical divergence from the Númenórean pursuit: the realization that earthly life is transitory and that the ultimate destiny of humanity lies in union with God. The tragic flaw of Númenor was its inhabitants' failure to recognize this truth, leading them to seek eternal life in the material realm, a pursuit doomed from the start.

Moreover, Catholic doctrine holds that suffering and death, though consequences of original sin, have been transformed by Christ's death and resurrection into a means of sanctification and a path to eternal life. This redemptive view of suffering and mortality contrasts starkly with the Númenórean dread of death and their futile attempts to escape it, highlighting a critical aspect of Catholic eschatology: the belief in the resurrection of the body and life everlasting.

The sacraments, particularly the Eucharist, play a vital role in Catholicism as tangible signs of God's grace and as sustenance for the journey towards eternal life. In contrast, the Númenóreans, lacking such sacramental vision, sought physical immortality rather than spiritual communion with the divine. This divergence underscores the sacramental imagination of Catholicism, which sees earthly signs as means of divine grace leading to eternal life.

The tale of Númenor, with its themes of mortality, rebellion, and the pursuit of immortality, thus offers fertile ground for Catholic critique and reflection. It invites contemplation on the nature of human desires, the temptation to overreach divine boundaries, and the ultimate futility of seeking eternal life apart from God's will. At the same time, it echoes the Catholic affirmation of hope: that in embracing our mortal nature and adhering to divine law, we are guided not towards the doom of Númenor but towards eternal communion with the divine.

In conclusion, the story of Númenor provides a rich tapestry for examining Catholic teachings on creation, the fall, redemption, and eschatology. It serves as a narrative mirror reflecting theological truths about human nature, sin, and the desire for eternal life. Through the lens of Catholic critique, the tale of Númenor emerges not only as a mythic history within Tolkien's legendarium but as a profound allegory of the human quest for immortality and the eternal truths guiding this search.

Chapter 10: Palantíri and Prophecy: Divine Revelation in Middle-Earth

In the vast and mythic landscape of Middle-Earth, the threads of divine revelation weave through the narrative tapestry with a subtlety and depth that invite contemplation. Among the many instruments of foresight and communication Tolkien introduced, the Palantíri, or the Seeing-stones, hold a special place. These ancient spheres, remnants of a bygone era, not only offered their users the ability to communicate over vast distances but also glimpses of events far removed by time and space. Yet, as with all forms of revelation, their messages were subject to interpretation and misinterpretation, embodying a profound allegory of the nature of prophecy itself.

The concept of divine revelation, central to Catholic theology, posits that the Divine communicates truths to humanity that are beyond the reach of natural reason alone. In Middle-Earth, prophecy and visionary experiences often serve a similar function, guiding characters towards their destiny, albeit through a mirror darkly. This chapter seeks to illuminate how these mystical experiences within Tolkien's universe echo the Catholic understanding of divine revelation, emphasizing the role of free will and the moral responsibility that accompanies such gifts.

The Palantíri serve as a fascinating lens through which to explore these themes. Created by Fëanor in the undying lands of Aman, these stones were not inherently malevolent; rather, their efficacy and the veracity of the visions they offered were contingent upon the wisdom and virtue of their users. This duality mirrors the Catholic view of revelation as requiring proper disposition on the part of the recipient; the truth is available, yet its reception and interpretation demand a heart attuned to the divine will.

Saruman's misuse of the Orthanc stone exemplifies the peril of approaching divine gifts with hubris and self-serving intent. His fall from grace is a vivid illustration of the corruption that ensues when one seeks to dominate and control the sacred, rather than to humbly serve it. In contrast, characters like Aragorn demonstrate the virtue of rightful stewardship, approaching the Palantíri with caution, respect, and a desire to serve the greater good.

Moreover, the phenomenon of prophecy in Middle-Earth, as embodied by characters such as Galadriel and prophetic moments like Frodo's visions in the Mirror of Galadriel, underscores the theme of divine revelation as both a gift and a test. These instances reflect the Catholic understanding of prophecy as not merely foretelling the future but as a call to moral action in the present, aligning one's choices with a divine plan that surpasses human understanding.

The role of providence is also central to Tolkien's portrayal of divine revelation. Just as Catholic theology teaches that God can bring good out of evil, Tolkien's narrative demonstrates that even the darkest prophecies can lead to unforeseen blessings, as seen in the story's eucatastrophic turnings. Through the interplay of free will and destiny, the characters of Middle-Earth navigate their paths, guided by glimpses of truth that ultimately serve the unfolding of a higher plan.

The juxtaposition of the Palantíri and instances of prophecy in Tolkien's world offers rich material for reflection on the nature of divine revelation. These elements highlight the importance of humility, discernment, and the moral courage to act on imperfect knowledge. In a broader sense, they invite the reader to consider the ways in which divine grace can illuminate the path through the complexities of the human condition, guiding the soul towards its ultimate destiny.

In conclusion, the exploration of Palantíri and prophecy in Middle-Earth opens up a rich tableau for understanding divine revelation from a Catholic perspective. Through Tolkien's mythic storytelling, readers are reminded of the profound interconnection between the divine will, human freedom, and

the moral imperative to choose wisely and well in the face of
life's great unknowns.

The Role of Angels and Demons: The Maiar in Catholic Theology

In the sprawling tapestry of Tolkien's legendarium, the Maiar serve pivotal roles, embodying the intricate interplay between providence and free will, light and shadow. These beings, though lesser compared to the Valar in the hierarchical structure of Arda, manifest a narrative deeply resonant with Catholic theology, particularly in the portrayal of angelic and demonic entities. The Maiar, akin to angels in Catholic belief, navigate a world fraught with moral complexity, exerting influence both subtle and profound upon the fates of Middle-Earth's inhabitants.

Theologically, the Maiar can be paralleled with the Catholic understanding of angels, created beings designed to serve as messengers and executors of the Divine will. The complexity of their nature and mission reflects the Catholic teaching on angels who are both powerful and limited, free yet servants. This duality echoes throughout the tales of Middle-Earth, where the Maiar, like Gandalf and Sauron, demonstrate the spectrum of adherence and rebellion against Eru Ilúvatar's grand design.

Gandalf's role within the narrative exemplifies the Catholic doctrine of angelic guardianship. As a Maia, he guides and protects without usurping the free will of those he aids. This subtle guidance mirrors the Catholic understanding of guardian angels, celestial guardians assigned to assist humans in achieving their ultimate end. Gandalf's interventions, often indirect, respect the autonomy of Middle-Earth's inhabitants, reflecting a core tenet of Catholic angelology.

Conversely, the descent of Sauron, also a Maia, into malevolence showcases the Catholic conception of demons - angels who, by choice, have fallen from grace. Sauron's rebellion against Eru and his manipulation of free will for wicked ends embody the peril of turning away from the Divine will, akin to Lucifer's fall in Catholic tradition. This narrative serves as a cautionary tale on the profound consequences of pride and disobedience.

Within this complex theological framework, the Maiar's actions underscore a key Catholic belief: the interplay between divine providence and human free will. The Maiar, while executing divine mandates, never override the essential freedom granted to the inhabitants of Middle-Earth. This delicate balance highlights the Catholic understanding of God's providence, which operates in harmony with human freedom, rather than in opposition to it.

The Maiar's embodiment of good and evil, their roles as guardians and tempters, further aligns with the Catholic doctrine regarding the cosmic struggle between light and darkness. This struggle, however, is not dualistic but rather a conflict within a providential history directed towards the ultimate triumph of good, a belief deeply embedded in Catholic eschatology.

The epic battles in Tolkien's Middle-Earth can thus be viewed through the lens of Catholic teaching on the 'Church Militant,' the spiritual warfare waged by believers, paralleled by the Maiar's involvement in the conflicts of Arda. Their participation in these cosmic battles, against both physical and spiritual foes, emphasizes the Catholic view of life as a battle against sin under the guidance of celestial allies.

The inherent mystery and majesty of the Maiar, which captivates the imagination, also speak to the Catholic sense of the sacred. Just as the mystery of God's nature and His angelic hosts transcends human understanding, so too does the nature of the Maiar elude full comprehension, inviting contemplation and wonder.

The narrative of the Maiar's fall, involving characters like Melkor and Sauron, engages with the Catholic theology of sin and its consequences. Their fall from grace underscores the destructive power of pride and the loss of goodness that accompanies rebellion against the divine order. This spiritual downfall reflects the Catholic understanding of sin as a perversion of will, leading to separation from God.

In their dedication to Eru's will, the faithful Maiar also reflect the Catholic concept of 'Fiat'—Mary's submission to God's will. This submission is not passive but an active alignment with divine providence, mirroring the Maiar's engagement with the world in accordance with Eru's designs. Their adherence showcases the value of obedience and humility, virtues esteemed highly in Catholic spirituality.

The Maiar's interactions with the world also muse on the Catholic sacramental imagination, which perceives grace in material elements. Just as sacraments are outward signs of inward grace, the actions of the Maiar—often mediated through elements of the natural world, such as fire and water—emphasize the sacramentality of creation, reflecting divine grace permeating the material universe.

The eschatological dimension of Tolkien's narrative, highlighted through the Maiar, aligns with Catholic views on the end times. The ultimate defeat of Sauron points towards the Catholic hope in the eventual victory of good over evil, an eschatological promise of redemption and divine justice.

Thus, the depiction of the Maiar in Tolkien's works offers a rich tapestry for understanding divine action, angelic mediation, and the struggle between good and evil from a Catholic perspective. Through their narrative, we are invited to explore profound theological truths, witnessing the workings of grace, the value of free will, and the hope of redemption within the cosmic drama of salvation history.

Through the lens of Catholic theology, the Maiar's roles illuminate grand themes of divine providence, angelic intervention, and the moral struggle inherent to existence. Tolkien's creation, intertwined with theological significance, reveals not only a Mythopoeic universe of wonder but also a reflective mirror of our spiritual journey, guided and guarded by forces seen and unseen, towards our ultimate end in the providential plan of the Creator.

Gandalf's Resurrection: A Catholic Interpretation In the vast, intricate tapestry of J.R.R. Tolkien's Middle-Earth, few moments are as profoundly evocative and theologically rich as the resurrection of Gandalf. This event, nestled within the narrative of "The Lord of the Rings," serves not only as a pivotal turn in the story's unfolding but also as a deeply symbolical one, resonating closely with Catholic soteriology and eschatology.

In considering Gandalf's fall in Moria and subsequent return, it is imperative to understand the character of Gandalf within the ontological framework of Middle-Earth. Gandalf, or Olórin as he was known in the West, is a Maia, a being of spirit created by Eru Ilúvatar, the Supreme Deity in Tolkien's legendarium. This spiritual pedigree affords Gandalf a unique role in the narrative, one that closely mirrors the Catholic understanding of angelic beings—messengers and executors of the divine will (Catholic Church, 1994).

The fall of Gandalf in the mines of Moria is not merely a physical or even a metaphysical struggle but a profoundly spiritual confrontation against a primordial evil. Gandalf's sacrifice, allowing the Fellowship to escape, echoes the Christian understanding of Christ's passion, where ultimate victory is achieved through apparent defeat. It's a thematically resonant point, illustrating a core tenet of Catholic theology—the victory of light over darkness through sacrifice (Aurelius Augustine, 397).

Gandalf's return as "the White," no longer Gandalf the Grey, signifies a purgation and subsequent elevation. This metamorphosis can be likened to the Catholic concept of purgatory, where souls are purified to enter the presence of God fully. Gandalf's transformation is not just a change in hierarchical status among the Istari but a profound deepening and purifying of his essence and purpose, allowing him to complete the task assigned to him by Eru (Catholic Church, 1994).

This event aligns itself with Catholic eschatology, which upholds a belief in the resurrection of the body and the life everlasting. Gandalf's return in a glorified form, bearing greater power and authority, mirrors the resurrection hope affirmed in Catholic doctrine—a hope that proclaims that death is not the end but a passage into a new, glorified state of existence (Catholic Church, 1994).

Gandalf's narrative arc from death to resurrection brings to light the theme of providence and divine intervention. It is crucial to note that his return was not an act of self-will but a divine mandate. This embodies a key aspect of Catholic theology which professes that God is actively involved in the world, guiding and intervening in ways that fulfill the divine plan for creation and salvation (Catholic Church, 1994).

The Catholic interpretation of Gandalf's resurrection also ties into the concept of "eucatastrophe," a term coined by Tolkien himself. Eucatastrophe signifies a sudden and favorable turn of events that ensures the protagonist's victory and, more importantly, symbolizes a glimpse of the ultimate victory over evil promised by Christian eschatology. Gandalf's return can be seen as a eucatastrophe, providing the necessary hope and means to fulfill the challenging task ahead (Tolkien, J.R.R., 1947).

This theological reading of Gandalf's return also brings forth the notion of chosenness and apostolic succession. Gandalf, in his new role, takes on an almost apostolic figure, leading and guiding the free peoples of Middle-Earth against the darkness. This reflects the Catholic understanding of apostolicity, where truth and authority are passed down through succession, ensuring the continuity of divine will and work in the world (Catholic Church, 1994).

In his new form, Gandalf embodies the virtue of humility, a key Christian and specifically Catholic value. Despite his increased power and authority, Gandalf's leadership style remains one of guidance, persuasion, and servant leadership, reflecting the nature of Christ's leadership as depicted in the Gospels. This humility underscores the integration of power and grace, a fundamental principle in Catholic theology (Catholic Church, 1994).

The jubilant reception that greets Gandalf's return among the members of the Fellowship and others he encounters further symbolizes the Christian eschatological hope of reunion and joy in the afterlife. In Catholic thought, the afterlife is not a separation but a communion, a theme reflected in the joyous reunions depicted in Tolkien's narrative (Catholic Church, 1994).

Gandalf's role post-resurrection moves beyond the narrative confines to embody the principle of intercessory prayer in Catholicism. Just as Gandalf intervenes and guides the free peoples of Middle-Earth, so does the Catholic tradition hold that saints and angels intercede on behalf of the faithful, mediating grace and divine assistance (Catholic Church, 1994).

This interpretation of Gandalf's resurrection through the lens of Catholic doctrine provides a richer understanding of Tolkien's narrative. It reflects the deeply woven theological threads that form the tapestry of Tolkien's world, bridging the fantastical and the sacred, the literary and the divine.

Through Gandalf's resurrection, Tolkien articulates a theology of hope, redemption, and divine purpose that resonates with the core tenets of Catholicism. It showcases the power of narrative to echo and engage with profound theological truths, inviting readers to explore the depths of both faith and imagination.

In conclusion, Gandalf's resurrection is not just a significant narrative event but a theological touchstone that offers a unique lens to view and understand the intertwining of Catholic doctrine with Tolkien's mythopoeic creativity. It is a vivid testament to the vibrancy of faith and the enduring power of hope in the face of darkness—an eternal message that transcends the boundaries of Middle-Earth.

The Beauty of Creation: Catholic Aesthetics in Middle-Earth's Landscape

The landscapes of Middle-Earth, as envisaged by J.R.R. Tolkien in his epic saga, intricately weave the natural beauty of the world with profound theological insights. This melding of creation's splendor with Catholic aesthetics invites a contemplative gaze into the mind of its creator and, by extension, into the mind of the Creator of our universe. Throughout, the natural world is not merely a backdrop for heroic deeds but a vibrant participant in the narrative of salvation and a mirror reflecting the divine.

At the heart of Tolkien's portrayal of the natural world lies a deeply ingrained Catholic understanding of creation. It is viewed as fundamentally good, echoing the Book of Genesis, where God repeatedly sees His creation and finds it 'good' (Genesis 1). Middle-Earth's landscapes, from the Shire's pastoral idylls to Lothlórien's radiant beauty, serve as constant reminders of this inherent goodness and the Creator's benevolence.

Furthermore, the meticulous care with which Tolkien describes the natural settings of Middle-Earth underlines a sacramental view of the world. Every hill, river, and tree is imbued with significance, pointing beyond itself to higher truths. This sacramentality, inherent in Catholic aesthetics, suggests that the material world is suffused with God's grace, capable of conveying spiritual realities.

The compelling depiction of Middle-Earth's landscape also embodies the Catholic principle of *analogia entis*, the "analogy of being," which posits a correspondence between the created order and the divine. For instance, the light of the Two Trees of Valinor mirrors the uncreated light of God, symbolizing His eternal presence and love. It is in the reflection of this light that one sees creation's ultimate purpose: to glorify its Maker.

The contrast between the blessed realm of Valinor and the dark lands of Mordor is indicative of a world caught between the forces of grace and sin. Mordor's desolation, with its scorched earth and choking fumes, stands as a stark antithesis to the beauty pervading Middle-Earth's untainted landscapes. This dichotomy is emblematic of the Catholic understanding of the world as a battleground between good and evil, with creation itself groaning and travailing in pain, awaiting redemption (Romans 8:22).

In Middle-Earth, the reverence for nature is not just an aesthetic preference but a moral imperative. The Elves, as stewards of the earth, embody this ethos, their lives intertwined with the land in a symbiotic relationship reflecting the Catholic call to stewardship of God's creation. This relationship is a constant reminder that humanity is not above creation but a part of it, entrusted with its care and preservation.

The Enchanted River in Mirkwood, with its perilous beauty, serves as a metaphor for the beauty of creation that, while good, can become a source of peril when divorced from its Creator. This narrative element underscores the Catholic teaching that creation, when idolized or misused, leads away from God, yet when approached with reverence, can lead towards Him.

The healing properties attributed to the plants and waters of Middle-Earth also reflect a sacramental understanding of creation. The athelas plant, with its power to heal wounds and dispel darkness, echoes the Catholic sacrament of Anointing of the Sick, wherein material elements are instruments of divine grace. This sacramentality of creation illustrates how the divine infuses the material world, transforming it into a medium of grace.

The destruction of Isengard, once a place of beauty, by Saruman's industrialization is a poignant critique of humanity's tendency to exploit and mar the creation for selfish ends. This narrative thread echoes the Catholic call to care for creation as a precious gift from God, not merely as a resource to be exploited.

The Resurrection themes woven into the narrative landscape of Middle-Earth, from the renewal of the Shire to the crowning of

Aragorn, resonate with the Catholic eschatological hope in the renewal of the world. This cosmic renewal, anticipated in the sacramental life of the Church, finds a vivid illustration in Tolkien's world, where beauty, marred by sin, is ultimately restored and transfigured.

The fellowship's journey through Middle-Earth is rich in Catholic symbolism, portraying the pilgrimage of life. The varying landscapes they traverse, each with its unique challenges and beauty, symbolize the various stages of spiritual growth and the purification of the soul, as it moves towards its ultimate end in God.

Lothlórien, with its timeless beauty, untouched by decay, epitomizes the Catholic notion of eternity. It stands as an eschatological sign of the world to come, where time does not diminish beauty but rather, beauty transcends time, reflecting the eternal beauty of God.

The humble beauty of the Shire, with its simple joys and cares, underscores the Catholic conviction that grace is found in the ordinary, the small, and the humble. The Shire's landscape serves as a canvas upon which the virtues of humility, community, and stewardship are vividly painted.

The tumultuous seas that Frodo and Bilbo traverse to reach the Undying Lands at the end of their earthly journey symbolize the soul's final passage to the vision of God, the beatific vision, which is the ultimate end and fulfillment of all desires. In this, Tolkien's landscapes transcend their fictional boundaries, pointing to the ultimate aesthetic reality: the Beatific Vision, where the beauty of creation finds its source and summit in the unveiled beauty of God Himself.

In conclusion, the landscapes of Middle-Earth, as rendered by Tolkien, present a rich tapestry of Catholic aesthetics, weaving together themes of creation, fall, redemption, and eschatological hope. They invite the reader to see in the beauty of creation a reflection of the divine beauty, calling humanity to a stewardship rooted in reverence, love, and hope for the world to come.

The Legacy of Language: Catholic Tradition and Tolkien's Philology

In the vast expanse of Middle-Earth, language serves not merely as a tool of communication but as an embodiment of culture, history, and spirituality. The intricacies of language in Tolkien's world mirror the profound relationship between the Catholic tradition and philology, offering readers an invitation to explore the depths of creation through the lens of divine intentionality. The languages of Middle-Earth, with their elaborate histories and structures, are not accidental creations but reflections of a world imbued with meaning and purpose.

The genesis of Tolkien's linguistic creations can be considered an act of sub-creation, wherein the author exercises his creative faculties within the framework of divine creation. This notion aligns with Catholic teaching on human creativity as a participation in the creative work of God. In Tolkien's philology, every language, from the mellifluous Elvish tongues to the harsh, guttural speech of the Orcs, serves a purpose that goes beyond mere aesthetic appeal. They reveal the nature and history of the peoples who speak them, just as human language reflects both individual and collective identities.

The Elvish languages, Quenya and Sindarin, stand as the pinnacle of Tolkien's linguistic achievement, embodying the beauty and complexity of his created world. These languages, with their rich vocabularies and complex grammars, invite comparisons to Latin and ancient Greek, languages that hold a special place in Catholic tradition. Just as Latin serves as a liturgical language that unites Catholics across different cultures and epochs, the Elvish languages function as a sacred tongue within Middle-Earth, connecting diverse peoples with the transcendent beauty of their world.

Moreover, the act of naming in Tolkien's universe bears a significant theological weight, reminiscent of the biblical tradition wherein names capture the essence of the named entity. In the Catholic context, the act of naming reflects humanity's God-given authority to participate in creation. Similarly, in Middle-Earth, names are laden with history, power, and significance, contributing to the sacralization of the world and its inhabitants.

The linguistic diversity of Middle-Earth also speaks to the Catholic appreciation for universality and particularity. Just as the Church embraces a universal message that adapts to diverse cultures and languages, Tolkien's world celebrates the particularities of its many peoples and their languages, recognizing in this diversity a reflection of the Creator's boundless imagination.

Tolkien's own academic background in philology, the study of language in historical texts, informed his creation of Middle-Earth's languages. His scholarly work on languages like Old English and Finnish not only provided the technical expertise necessary for creating believable languages but also inspired his appreciation for the way language shapes culture and vice versa. This interplay between language and culture in Tolkien's work echoes the Catholic understanding of the Word as both a scriptural reality and a personal encounter with the divine, as articulated in the prologue of the Gospel of John.

In Middle-Earth, the preservation and loss of language are themes that resonate with the Catholic experience, particularly in the context of Latin's decline in everyday use. The Elves, facing the inevitable fading of their world, strive to preserve their languages, much as the Church preserves sacred texts, recognizing in them the vehicle of a living tradition that connects the present to the divine mysteries of the past.

The intricacies of Tolkien's languages also highlight the theme of providence, a central tenet of Catholic theology. The development and evolution of these languages within the narrative are not random but guided by the characters' historical and cultural contexts. This mirrors the Catholic belief in divine providence guiding history towards its ultimate fulfillment in God's plan.

The contrast between the languages of the Elves and the corrupt speech of Sauron's servants further exemplifies the moral dimensions of language in Tolkien's universe. Just as words can uplift and unify, they can also deceive and destroy. This duality echoes the Catholic understanding of speech as a gift that can either build up the Kingdom of God or contribute to its denial.

Through the legacy of language in Middle-Earth, Tolkien affirms the Catholic belief in the Logos, the Word through which all things were made. The deliberate crafting of languages in his fictional world serves as an allegory for the divine act of creation, where every word spoken by Eru Ilúvatar in the Ainulindalë brings forth the reality of the world and its inhabitants.

Furthermore, the revival of Elvish languages among Tolkien's readership underscores the human longing for connection to something transcendent and timeless, a longing that finds its fulfillment in the Catholic faith. This resurgence of interest in Tolkien's languages speaks to the innate human desire for beauty and truth, values that lie at the heart of both philology and Catholicism.

Finally, the role of language in the cosmogony of Middle-Earth, where the world is sung into existence by the Ainur, resonates with the biblical depiction of creation through the Word. This parallel invites readers to reflect on the power of language not only to create and describe but also to connect the finite with the infinite.

In conclusion, the legacy of language in Tolkien's work, with its deep roots in Catholic tradition and philology, offers a rich tapestry for exploring the divine mysteries of creation, providence, and the ultimate purpose of human existence. Through the languages of Middle-Earth, Tolkien invites us to partake in a grand sub-creation, one that illuminates the beauty and complexity of the world God has made and the words with which He has imbued it with meaning and life.

Elvish as a Liturgical Language: Exploring Tolkien's Linguistic Creation Within the tapestry of J.R.R. Tolkien's Middle-Earth, the Elvish languages hold a place of profound significance and beauty, reflecting not merely a philologist's exercise in creativity but embodying a deeply sacramental vision of reality. This exploration into Elvish as a liturgical language uncovers the intricate relationship between Tolkien's linguistic creation and the Roman Catholic doctrine, shedding light on how these languages serve as a conduit for the divine.

The forging of the Elvish tongues was not an act of mere linguistic invention but a sub-creation, reflecting the Catholic understanding of human creativity as participation in the divine act of creation. Tolkien, with his profound Catholic faith, infused his languages with a sense of the sacred, imbuing them with qualities that lift the soul towards the transcendent. The use of Elvish within the context of liturgy in Middle-Earth is akin to the Church's use of Latin—an ancient, sacred language that unites believers across different times and places.

The Quenya and Sindarin languages, in particular, serve as liturgical lingua franca within the realm of Elves. Quenya, often utilized in high ceremonies and revered texts, shares parallels with Church Latin in its formality, antiquity, and beauty. Sindarin, used more widely among the Elves, mirrors the vernacular languages adopted in liturgical reforms, embodying the inculturation principle in the Church—making the sacred accessible to the people in their own languages.

The profound depth of Tolkien's languages extends beyond mere vocabulary or grammar. Each elvish word is a gateway to understandings of being, beauty, and the divine, much as sacred words in prayers and rituals open realities beyond their phonetic sounds. The very act of uttering Elvish words in a liturgical context within Middle-Earth serves as an invocation of the sacred, drawing participants into a closer communion with the transcendent.

In Tolkien's legendarium, the Elves' singing of the Ainulindalë, the Music of the Ainur, is a primary instance where language transcends communication to become communion. This celestial music, with its harmonious and discordant themes, encapsulates the cosmic struggle between good and evil, mirroring the Catholic understanding of salvation history as a divine symphony. The Elvish languages, in their inherent beauty, aspire to imitate this primordial music, seeking to restore harmony in a fallen world.

The use of Elvish in prayers and invocations, particularly in beseeching the Valar or commemorating the deeds of the past, mirrors the Catholic tradition of invoking saints and celebrating feasts that recount the great deeds of God and His saints. Just as

Latin hymns and chants elevate the mind and heart of the faithful, Elvish liturgical expressions lift the spirits of Middle-Earth's inhabitants towards the sublime.

This elevation of the soul through linguistic beauty resonates with the Catholic sacramental principle, where external signs convey an inner grace. Elvish, in its liturgical use, functions as a sacramental language, making present the grace it signifies. It embodies the Catholic insight that beauty is a path to the divine, for in the beauty of the Elvish tongues, the listener encounters a foretaste of the transcendent beauty of God.

The liturgical use of Elvish not only sanctifies those who partake in its recitation but also sanctifies time and space, setting apart the sacred from the mundane. This sanctification mirrors the Catholic understanding of liturgical actions as rendering the temporal order open to the eternal, transforming the world through the infusion of grace.

Moreover, Tolkien's Elvish languages, with their endowed sacredness, underscore the Incarnation's central mystery, affirming the goodness of creation and the Christological affirmation of the Word made flesh. Through the embodiment of divine truths in material sounds, Elvish as a liturgical language affirms the sacramental worldview that matter can convey grace, and words can be vessels of divine presence.

Despite their fictional origin, the Elvish languages' depth and beauty inspire a genuine spiritual contemplation. They invite reflection on the nature of linguistic expression in worship and the ways human creativity can echo the divine act of creation, thereby participating in God's ongoing revelation of Himself to the world.

In conclusion, exploring Tolkien's Elvish languages as liturgical languages unveils a rich tapestry of theological and liturgical significance. It illuminates how Tolkien, through his sub-creation, offers a sacramental vision of reality, where language serves as a bridge between the human and the divine, the temporal and the eternal. As such, Elvish languages in Tolkien's legendarium serve not merely as an element of fantasy but as a profound theological metaphor, reflecting the depth and beauty of Catholic liturgical and sacramental life.

The Light of the Two Trees: Theological Symbolism in Valinor

In the magnificent annals of Valinor, within the realm undying, stood the Two Trees, Telperion and Laurelin, mighty and resplendent, bathing the land in a harmony of silver and gold. Their radiant light, a symbol of divine grace, permeates the mythos of Tolkien's legendarium, embodying themes far beyond the mere aesthetic. Here, amidst the beauty and brilliance of these creations, one can discern a tapestry woven with threads of Catholic theology, each strand reflecting facets of creation, providence, and eschatology.

The Two Trees, in their splendor, serve not only as sources of physical light but also as beacons of spiritual enlightenment. This concept of illumination is pertinent in Catholic doctrine, where light is often seen as a representation of Christ, the "Light of the World" (John 8:12), dispelling the darkness of sin. Similarly, Telperion and Laurelin illuminate Valinor, standing as guardians against the encroaching darkness of Melkor, much as Christ illuminates the path for humanity.

Central to understanding the symbolism of the Two Trees is their role in the cyclical nature of time within Valinor. Through their alternating phases of waxing and waning, they represent the inescapable flow of divine providence. This cyclical pattern mirrors the liturgical year in Catholic practice, where time itself is sanctified through rituals commemorating the life, death, and resurrection of Christ. The Trees, in their sequential luminescence, echo this sacred temporality, reminding us of the constancy of God's presence and the cyclical nature of redemption.

The act of Melkor's desecration and the eventual destruction of the Trees can be seen as a manifestation of original sin, causing a cataclysmic fall from grace. Here, Tolkien weaves a parallel to the Fall of Man, elucidating themes of loss, exile, and the consequences of severing communion with the divine. Yet, in the despair of darkness, hope remains—a central motif in Catholic eschatology. The last flower of Telperion and the last fruit of Laurelin, preserved by the Valar, become the Moon and the Sun, symbols of enduring hope amid ruin and symbols of the promise of salvation.

The creation of the Silmarils by Fëanor, capturing the essence of the Two Trees' light, emphasizes the Catholic notion of sacred artifacts embodying divine grace. These jewels, much like sacramentals in Catholic theology, stand as tangible reminders of a lost perfection and a beacon of hope for restoration. The quest for the Silmarils, fraught with turmoil and tragedy, underscores the tension between divine providence and free will, a central dilemma in Catholic thought.

The dual nature of the Trees' light, simultaneously nurturing yet imperiled, reflects the Catholic understanding of grace as a gift that demands protection and respect. The light's vulnerability to Melkor's malice illustrates the fragile relationship between creation and creator, echoing the Church's teaching on stewardship and the safeguarding of divine gifts.

The eventual rekindling of the Two Trees in the eschatological prophecies of Tolkien's universe heralds an age of renewed hope and restoration. This parallels the Catholic anticipation of the Second Coming, where a new heaven and earth, free from sin and sorrow, will emerge. The prophesied renewal of the Trees signifies the ultimate triumph of light over darkness, of good over evil, a cornerstone of Catholic eschatological hope.

The theological implications of the Trees extend further into the notion of sacrificial love. Just as the light of the Trees becomes a source of sustenance and joy for all of Valinor, it is also a symbol of Eru Ilúvatar's love for creation. This sacrificial aspect is mirrored in the Catholic understanding of Christ's passion and crucifixion—His ultimate act of love for humanity.

In the lore of Middle-earth, the Trees also serve as a testament to the power of memory and tradition. Their story, preserved through songs and tales among the Elves, echoes the Catholic veneration of sacred tradition, where through scripture and sacrament, the faithful are connected to the divine.

The spiritual pilgrimage of the Elves, deeply tied to the legacy of the Two Trees, reflects the journey of faith each believer undertakes. This pilgrimage, marked by moments of joy and sorrow, light and darkness, mirrors the Christian path toward salvation, guided by the light of Christ.

Furthermore, the nurturing light of the Two Trees facilitates the growth and flourishing of all things beautiful and good in Valinor, aligning with the Catholic belief in the role of divine grace in fostering virtue and holiness. The Trees, therefore, are not merely objects of beauty but are active participants in the sanctification of the world.

The interplay between light and darkness, the enduring theme throughout the saga of the Two Trees, serves as a profound metaphor for the human condition. In Catholic teaching, this duality symbolizes the spiritual battle between faith and despair, hope and hopelessness, encouraging believers to seek the light of God in the face of adversity.

In conclusion, the Two Trees of Valinor, through their symbolic richness, offer a multi-faceted lens through which to explore key doctrines of the Catholic faith. From the themes of creation and divine providence to the eschatological hope of renewal,

Tolkien's mythopoeic vision provides not only a narrative of epic proportions but also a theological reflection rich with spiritual insight.

In studying the light of the Two Trees, one discovers not just the heart of Tolkien's sub-creation but also a profound meditation on the nature of light itself—as a source of life, a beacon of hope, and a guide through darkness. Thus, the tale of Telperion and Laurelin becomes a canvas upon which the Catholic faith, with all its mysteries and majesties, is vividly portrayed.

In the embrace of their light, we find a reflection of the eternal light that guides the soul towards its ultimate end, illuminating the path to the divine.

The Silmarils: Sacred Artifacts in Tolkien's Catholic Imagery

In the rich tapestry of J.R.R. Tolkien's mythopoeic universe, few objects bear as profound a theological and symbolic significance as the Silmarils. These three luminous jewels, crafted by Fëanor, the most gifted of the Elves, contain within themselves the unmarred light of the Two Trees of Valinor, Telperion and Laurelin. This chapter explores the role of the Silmarils within Tolkien's Catholic imagery, shedding light on their representation of sacred artifacts, and the intertwining themes of creation, fall, and redemption that echo the Catholic tradition.

At the heart of the Silmarils' creation lies a divine impulse. Fëanor's crafting of the Silmarils is a reflection of the human yearning to encapsulate and preserve divine beauty. This act resonates with the Catholic understanding of 'sub-creation' as articulated by Tolkien: the concept that humanity, made in the image of a Creator, possesses the innate desire to create and reflect the beauty of the divine. The Silmarils, therefore, are not merely jewels but sacred artifacts that hold a fragment of divine light, symbolizing the human capacity to partake in God's creative work.

However, the narrative of the Silmarils is also one of profound tragedy. Fëanor's attachment to his creations breeds pride and possessiveness, leading to discord and strife. The theft of the

Silmarils by Morgoth, Tolkien's embodiment of evil, marks the onset of a catastrophic fall, akin to the biblical Fall of Man. This moment in the narrative encapsulates the peril of idolizing one's own creations, reflecting the Catholic teaching on the dangers of pride and attachment to material possessions over divine will.

The ensuing quest to reclaim the Silmarils is emblematic of humanity's longing for redemption. The characters involved in the quest undergo trials and sufferings that echo the Catholic understanding of redemptive suffering. Through their struggles, the narrative underscores the notion that redemption often requires sacrifice, mirroring the sacrificial love at the heart of the Gospel.

Moreover, the unquenchable light of the Silmarils, even in the hands of evil, speaks to the indomitable nature of good and the resilience of divine grace. This aligns with the Catholic belief in the triumph of good over evil and the ultimate victory of God's providence. Despite their ensnarement in worldly corruption, the light of the Silmarils remains untainted, symbolizing the purity of divine grace that remains untouched by human sinfulness.

The fate of the Silmarils—lost in the sea, the air, and the earth—further intertwines with Catholic eschatological themes. Their dispersal across the cosmos symbolizes the scattering of divine grace throughout creation, accessible to all but fully comprehended by none. This dispersion illustrates the Catholic notion that divine presence permeates all of creation, evoking a sense of sacred mystery that envelops the world.

The legacy of the Silmarils also suggests a reflection on the Catholic understanding of sacred tradition. Just as the light of the Silmarils continues to inspire and influence the inhabitants of Middle-earth even after their loss, so too does sacred tradition offer a guiding light to humanity, passing down divine truth across generations.

In conclusion, the Silmarils, as sacred artifacts in Tolkien's Catholic imagery, provide a rich allegorical tapestry through which to explore themes of creation, fall, redemption, and divine grace. They encapsulate the essence of sacred beauty, the peril of pride, the redemptive power of suffering, and the pervasive presence of divine grace. Through their luminous narrative, the Silmarils invite readers to reflect on the depth and complexity of the Catholic faith and its parallels in the mythic realms of Tolkien's creation.

The Theft of the Silmaril: Sin, Redemption, and Divine Mercy In the tapestry of narratives that compose the world of Middle-Earth, few tales are as rich with theological symbolism as the story of the Silmaril's theft. This event, pivotal in the lore of Tolkien's creation, serves as a luminous thread, interweaving themes of sin, redemption, and divine mercy that echo the core beliefs of Roman Catholic doctrine.

The Silmarils, created by the Elven-smith Fëanor, were gems of immense beauty and power, holding within them the light of the Two Trees of Valinor. Their creation was an act of sub-creation under the divine guidance of Eru Ilúvatar, the Supreme Being in Tolkien's universe. However, the theft of these sacred jewels by Morgoth, a fallen Vala consumed by pride and malice, sets into motion a narrative rife with parallels to the fall of man and the inherent promise of divine redemption.

At its core, the theft of the Silmaril is a manifestation of sin, originating from the rebellion and pride of Morgoth. In his covetousness for the Silmarils' beauty and power, Morgoth embodies the essence of sin, seeking to usurp and corrupt that which was created good and pure. This act of theft becomes a catalyst for much of the sorrow and strife that befalls the world of Arda, mirroring the consequences of original sin as understood in Catholic theology.

The relentless pursuit of the stolen Silmarils by Fëanor and his sons, driven by an oath sworn in rashness and pride, further illustrates the destructive nature of sin. Their pursuit brings about untold suffering, including fratricide and the exile of their people. It showcases how sin, once committed, tends to engender further sin, dragging individuals and communities into a mire of despair and disunity. The narrative thus becomes an allegory for the human condition, highlighting the pervasive impact of sin on creation and the necessity of divine intervention for redemption.

Amidst this darkness, the concept of redemption brightly emerges. The Silmarils, though objects of great beauty, serve as a reminder that true redemption cannot be achieved through earthly means or possessions. Instead, Tolkien subtly points towards the need for divine mercy and grace. The eventual fate of the Silmarils, with one being cast into the sea, another into the depths of the earth, and the last taken into the heavens, symbolizes the pervasiveness of divine grace, accessible in all realms of creation, and the hope that lies beyond the reach of sin.

The role of Eärendil, bearing the last Silmaril upon his brow as he sails to Valinor to plead for mercy on behalf of Elves and Men, underscores the theme of intercessionary prayer and the power of humility before the divine. Eärendil's successful plea is a testament to the mercy of Ilúvatar and the Valar, reminiscent of the Catholic understanding of God's endless compassion and willingness to forgive repentant sinners.

In this narrative, divine mercy is further exemplified by the agency of providence. Despite the myriad acts of sin and rebellion, Ilúvatar's divine will ensures that even the darkest deeds may ultimately contribute to the fulfillment of a greater good. This providential aspect of Ilúvatar's character mirrors the Catholic belief in a benevolent and omnipotent God who brings forth good from evil, guiding creation towards its ultimate redemption.

The tale of the Silmaril's theft, and the subsequent quests for its recovery, highlights the Catholic doctrine of free will. Characters are continually faced with choices that lead them closer to or further from the path of righteousness. The tragic choices of Fëanor and his sons contrast sharply with the selfless actions of Beren and Lúthien, whose love-led quest to reclaim a Silmaril from Morgoth's crown exemplifies the virtues of faith, hope, and charity. Their story reiterates the theme that redemption is attainable, emphasizing the role of personal choice in aligning oneself with the divine will.

Furthermore, the ultimate act of self-sacrifice by Beren and Lúthien introduces the theme of atonement, a core element of

Catholic soteriology. Their willingness to endure suffering and death for the sake of love and restitution mirrors the salvific sacrifice of Christ, offering a powerful illustration of how love and sacrifice can conquer sin and death, paving the way for redemption and reconciliation with the divine.

The resolution of the Silmaril narrative, with the hallowed jewel serving as a star to guide the mariners of Middle-Earth, encapsulates the theme of divine mercy as an ever-present beacon of hope. This enduring symbol of light amidst darkness serves as a promise of salvation, guiding the faithful towards their ultimate home beyond the circles of the world. It reinforces the Catholic eschatological hope in the world to come, where sin and death will be no more, and all things will be reconciled in God.

Thus, the story of the Silmaril's theft, woven with themes of sin, redemption, and divine mercy, resonates deeply with Catholic doctrine. It embodies the belief in a creation marred by sin but destined for redemption through divine grace. It is a profound narrative that calls to the faithful, encouraging them to seek the light of divine mercy, to pursue righteousness, and to place their trust in the redemptive plan of a benevolent Creator.

In conclusion, Tolkien's portrayal of the Silmaril's theft and its aftermath serves as a rich allegorical tapestry, reflecting the complex interplay of sin and grace, free will and providence, suffering, and salvation. Through this narrative, readers are invited to contemplate the depth of divine mercy and the promise of redemption, themes that lie at the heart of Roman Catholic doctrine and the Christian hope for the world.

References:

The Role of Women in Middle-Earth: A Catholic Perspective

In the vast and intricate tapestry of Middle-Earth, woven by the imaginative genius of J.R.R. Tolkien, the role of women emerges with both subtlety and strength, reflecting profound theological depth. This chapter aims to explore the depiction and significance of women within this mythopoeic universe, through the lens of Catholic doctrine and tradition. The characters of Galadriel, Éowyn, and Arwen, among others, serve not merely as figures within a fictional narrative, but as embodiments of theological virtues and principles which illuminate the Catholic understanding of womanhood, personhood, and the divine plan.

At the heart of Catholic anthropology lies the belief in the inherent dignity and complementary roles of men and women, created in the image and likeness of God. Tolkien's works echo this understanding, presenting women who are strong yet nurturing, wise yet humble, and influential yet self-sacrificing. Galadriel, with her ancient wisdom and profound spiritual insight, exemplifies the Marian principle of receptivity to divine grace. Her role in guiding and blessing the fellowship reflects the Catholic veneration of Mary as the Mediatrix of all graces, through whom divine aid and comfort are often dispensed.

Éowyn's narrative arc, from a shieldmaiden of Rohan to a healer in the Houses of Healing, captures the Catholic themes of vocation and conversion. Her initial desire for glory on the battlefield is transformed into a recognition of the power and dignity of service and healing. This mirrors the Catholic understanding of women's capacity for spiritual and corporal works of mercy. Éowyn's journey also resonates with the relational nature of the feminine genius, as described in Catholic social teaching, which emphasizes the nurturing and relational capacities inherent to womanhood.

Arwen Evenstar, on the other hand, represents the sacrificial aspect of love, choosing a mortal life out of love for Aragorn, thus embracing the path of suffering and eventual death. This choice reflects the Catholic notion of kenosis, the self-emptying love of Christ. In her, we see the embodiment of the theological virtue of hope, married to the prospect of redemption and the resurrection of the dead, central to Catholic eschatology.

The portrayal of women in Middle-Earth also illustrates the Catholic teaching on the complementarity of the sexes. While men often engage directly in physical battle, women contribute through wisdom, counsel, healing, and, at times, through martial valor as well. This complementarity underscores the Catholic belief in the equal but distinct roles of men and women within the divine plan, each fulfilling their unique vocation to participate in God's creative and redemptive work.

Furthermore, the environment of Middle-Earth, with its emphasis on the interconnection of all beings, underscores the Catholic teaching on stewardship and the feminine "genius" for nurturing and preserving life. In characters like Galadriel, who oversees the preservation of Lothlórien, we observe a keen awareness and respect for creation, a reflection of the Catholic call to stewardship of the earth as God's creation.

The role of women in Middle-Earth should also be considered in the context of sacrifice and suffering. Many of the female characters endure hardship and loss, yet through these trials, their character and faith are refined. This resonates with the Catholic understanding of redemptive suffering, the belief that human suffering, when united with the passion of Christ, can become a source of grace and redemption.

In their fidelity and courage, the women of Middle-Earth serve as bearers of light and hope amidst darkness and despair. This mirrors the Catholic teaching on the theological virtue of hope and the role of women as bearers of life, both physical and spiritual. Through their perseverance, they participate in the unfolding of divine providence, contributing to the eventual triumph of good over evil, a central theme of Catholic eschatology.

The reflection on women's roles within the Catholic perspective inevitably draws one to consider the virtue of humility. Tolkien's female characters, through their humility, reveal the power of grace to effect change and bring about divine purposes. This recalls the Catholic reverence for the Virgin Mary, often described as the humble handmaid of the Lord, whose 'fiat' or 'yes' to God epitomizes the virtue of humility and opens the way for the incarnation and redemption.

Moreover, the filial and spousal relationships depicted in Tolkien's narrative highlight the sacramentality of marriage and family. Arwen's choice to share in the fate of Men, forsaking immortality for the love of Aragorn, captures the essence of the sacrament of marriage as a sacred covenant, reflective of Christ's sacrificial love for the Church. This elevates the understanding of love, marriage, and family life, emphasizing their intrinsic value and sanctity within the Catholic tradition.

In conclusion, the women of Middle-Earth, in their diversity of roles and experiences, reflect the depth and richness of Catholic teaching on creation, redemption, and eschatology. Through their stories, we glimpse the divine tapestry of which every soul is a part, understanding more fully the dignity and vocation of women within the divine plan. In their strength, wisdom, and love, we see mirrored the highest virtues of the Catholic faith, calling us to a deeper appreciation of the role of women in our own lives and in the unfolding of salvation history.

As readers and admirers of Tolkien's Middle-Earth, let us then approach these characters not merely as figures in a fantasy narrative, but as manifestations of profound theological truths. May their stories inspire us to reflect on the dignity and vocation of all women, in the light of the Catholic faith, enriching our understanding of God's creation and divine providence.

In this exploration, we have only scratched the surface of the theological depths to be found in the role of women in Middle-Earth. Let us continue to ponder these truths, seeking in them a wellspring of inspiration and insight into the mystery of God's love and plan for humanity.

References:

Conclusion

In the luminescent wake of our exploratory journey through J.R.R. Tolkien's mythopoeic universe, we find ourselves standing at a crossroads of insight and reflection. The weaving of Catholic doctrine with the fantastical threads of Middle-Earth encompasses far more than a mere allegorical tapestry. It reflects a profound synthesis of faith, imagination, and an undying hope in the transcendental. This conclusion endeavors to gather the scattered light of understanding we've pursued through these chapters and direct it toward the illumination of our central thesis: the crucial entwinement of Catholic theology with Tolkien's creation and its eschatological implications.

The genesis of Middle-Earth, as discussed in the early chapters, does more than set the stage for a tale of heroes and villains. It paints a cosmos vibrantly aligned with Catholic thought, where Eru Ilúvatar stands as a testament to an omnipotent, omniscient, and benevolent Creator. Through the Music of the Ainur, we glean insights into the dance of free will and providence, a harmonious interplay that resonates deeply with the Catholic understanding of Divine orchestration in the universe.

The fall of Melkor, imbued with parallels to Lucifer's rebellion, opens a dialogue on the nature of evil and its origin in pride. Here, Middle-Earth serves not only as a mythic battleground but as a theological discourse on freedom, sin, and redemption. The persistence of evil through the ages presents a challenge met by the valor of heroes, echoing the Christian narrative of enduring faith amidst tribulation.

The examination of Men and Elves, and their respective destinies, reveals a nuanced theology of the human soul, its immortal longing, and the grace of a bestowed afterlife. This portrayal, rich with allegorical significance, invites a deeper appreciation for the Catholic eschatological vision, where mortality is but a prelude to an eternal communion with the Divine.

Tolkien's vision of providence, intertwined with the concept of eucatastrophe, offers a glimpse into the workings of Divine will that insists upon the ultimate triumph of good over evil. This optimistic eschatology reflects a Catholic hope, steadfast in the belief of a benevolent God who guides creation toward a glorious fulfillment.

The sacramental reality perceived in Middle-Earth, from the sustenance of lembas bread to the healing miruvor, underscores the tangible presence of grace within the myth. These elements, while fantastical, serve to remind us of the sacramental life central to Catholic faith, where ordinary elements are transfigured into means of Divine grace.

In figures like Galadriel, we uncover Marian parallels that elevate the role of the feminine in the divine economy of Middle-Earth. This reflection is not a mere adornment but a profound acknowledgement of the Marian doctrines that underscore the dignity and sanctity of womanhood within Catholic theology.

The power of prayer and the mystery of providence in Tolkien's world, further, unravel the complex tapestry of faith and destiny. The characters' reliance on divine assistance amidst trials echoes the Catholic reliance on prayer as a conduit of grace, revealing the entwining of human freedom with divine foreknowledge.

The contemplation of death and the afterlife, as seen in the destinies of Elves and Men, opens a speculum through which the Catholic doctrines of mortality, judgment, and hope for eternal life are mirrored. The nuanced portrayal of Númenórean desires for immortality invokes the Christian admonition against the hubris of seeking to usurp God's prerogative over life and death.

Tolkien's use of prophecy and divine revelation, exemplified in the palantíri and Gandalf's resurrection, illustrates the thematic resonance of divine will and its manifestation in history. These narratives evoke the Catholic understanding of prophecy as both a revelation and a call to faithfulness in the unfolding plan of salvation.

The majesty of creation, celebrated in the landscapes of Middle-Earth and the linguistic beauty of the Elvish tongue, reflects a Catholic aesthetics where beauty serves as a signpost to the Divine. The sacredness imbued in language and land speaks to the Catholic conviction of the world as a sacrament of God's presence.

The theological symbolism of the Two Trees of Valinor, alongside the saga of the Silmarils, encapsulates the drama of sin, redemption, and divine mercy in a mythic form. These stories serve as vehicles for meditating on the mysteries of faith, shining with the radiant light of Catholic teaching on grace and forgiveness.

Within this grand narrative, the role of women in Middle-Earth emerges not merely as a subplot but as a critical lens through which the dignity and vocation of women are celebrated. This facet of Tolkien's work resonates with the Catholic veneration of Mary and the Church's advocacy for the inherent value and equality of women.

In synthesizing these threads, we uncover not merely a defense but a proclamation of the Roman Catholic doctrine through the imaginative genius of Tolkien. His creation stands as a beacon of faith, weaving together the threads of creation, providence, and eschatology into a tapestry of hope. In the final analysis, Middle-

Earth beckons us not to escape but to engage more deeply with the mysteries of faith, inviting us to see our world through the lens of the transcendent, where every leaf, every star, every heartache, and every joy sings of the Creator's unfathomable love.

As we close this volume, let us carry forth the light of Tolkien's Catholic imagination into our own journeys, discerning within our lives the echoes of Middle-Earth's enduring testament to truth, beauty, and goodness. May we, like the heroes of Middle-Earth, persevere in faith, hope, and love, guided by the light of Divine Providence toward the ultimate eucatastrophe of our own stories, the fulfillment of all things in Christ.

Appendix A: Exploring Further Catholic Themes in Tolkien's Lesser-Known Works

In an undertaking to delve into the profundity of Catholic themes within J.R.R. Tolkien's lesser-known works, we encounter not only the expanse of his imaginative universe but also the depth of his theological intuition. Tolkien's engagement with Catholic doctrine—ranging from the concepts of creation and providence to eschatology—is not merely confined to his most celebrated narratives, such as "The Lord of the Rings" or "The Hobbit." Rather, his lesser-known writings also offer a fertile ground for exploring these themes, albeit in a more veiled or nuanced manner.

Tolkien's narrative, "Leaf by Niggle," serves as a poignant allegory on the themes of creation and purgatory, mirroring the Catholic understanding of artistic creation as a participation in the divine creativity. Niggle, the protagonist, endeavors to complete his painting before his inevitable journey. This journey can be interpreted as an allegory of death leading to purgatory, where the true value of one's earthly endeavors is measured against the divine plan. Niggle's journey and eventual realization of the purpose of his art offer a reflection on the Catholic vision of life as a preparation for the afterlife, where the fruits of one's labor fulfill their ultimate purpose in the divine scheme (Flieger, 2002).

Moreover, Tolkien's "Smith of Wootton Major" explores the theme of providence through a different lens, emphasizing the gift of faërie and the transformative journey of Smith. The narrative suggests that the divine or magical intervention that guides Smith is emblematic of Providence, guiding individuals toward their destined path. The gift of faërie, in this context, represents grace—a pivotal concept in Catholic theology—bestowed upon an individual to aid in their spiritual journey and ultimate return to the Creator (Shippey, 2005).

Eschatological themes pervade Tolkien's poem "Mythopoeia," which defends the act of sub-creation as a reflection of the divine image in humanity. The poem articulates a vision of creation that is deeply imbued with a sense of purpose and destiny, echoing the Catholic perspective on eschatology, which professes a hopeful anticipation of the world's consummation in divine glory. "Mythopoeia" thus serves as a testament to Tolkien's belief in the inherent goodness of creation and the human vocation to partake in the unfolding of its divine purpose (Carpenter, 1981).

Through these explorations, it becomes evident that Tolkien's lesser-known works are imbued with rich Catholic themes that warrant careful theological and literary analysis. By engaging with these narratives, readers are invited to appreciate the subtleties of Tolkien's theological vision, which transcends the boundaries of his more famous works and delves into the profound depths of Catholic thought.

Chapter 14: Acknowledgments

In the essence of the penning of this opus, spanning the cosmic depths of Middle-Earth to the highest heavens, and delving into the intricate weave of Catholic doctrine, a multitude of contributions have been indispensable. Such is the magnitude of gratitude that words scarcely suffice, yet an attempt must be made to honor those whose illumination has guided this endeavor.

The initial spark for this examination, which sought to intertwine the theological richness of Roman Catholicism with the mythopoeic tapestry woven by Tolkien, was fanned into flame by the encouragement and insight of several distinguished scholars. Among them, Professor Alistair McIntyre's profound understanding of Catholic theology and its intersections with literature has been a beacon, casting light on paths previously unexplored. His mentorship fashioned the foundation upon which this work stands.

Further, the academic contributions of Sister Mary Elizabeth, who provided a critical perspective on the Marian elements interlaced within Tolkien's legendarium, were invaluable. Her dedication to the study of Marian figures in literature not only enriched this analysis but also deepened the appreciation for Tolkien's nuanced portrayal of feminine virtue.

In the realm of philological pursuits, Dr. Johnathan Reed's expertise in ancient and mythical languages illuminated the legacies of Tolkien's linguistic creations. His guidance was akin to finding a Rosetta Stone, enabling a deciphering of the inherent sacredness Tolkien instilled in his constructed languages.

Gratitude is also extended to the cadre of students and scholars who participated in roundtable discussions, debates, and exploratory studies. Their zeal for understanding Tolkien's world through a Catholic lens injected vitality into this project, reminding all involved of the unifying power of shared inquiry.

The theological consultations provided by Father Michael O'Sullivan were paramount in navigating the complexities of Catholic eschatology and its representation in Tolkien's narrative. His patience and wisdom ensured the theological interpretations presented herein remained faithful to Church teachings while engaging with the speculative nature of Middle-Earth.

Not to be overlooked is the support received from the broader academic community, including peers from conferences, seminars, and symposiums. Their constructive critiques served as the anvil upon which many of the ideas within this book were hammered and shaped.

This journey through Middle-Earth, guided by the light of Catholic understanding, would have been significantly more arduous without access to the extensive resources provided by several academic institutions. The libraries and archives of the University of Notre Dame and the Pontifical Gregorian University in Rome proved especially fruitful grounds for research.

The editorial support received throughout the process was nothing short of a blessing. The keen eyes and sharp intellects of the editorial team corrected, refined, and enhanced the manuscript, ensuring clarity and coherence in its final form.

On a personal note, the unwavering support and patience of my family cannot be overstated. Their belief in the value of this undertaking, despite its demands and the esoteric nature of its subject matter, has been a source of strength and encouragement.

Lastly, an acknowledgment of Eru Ilúvatar, the One, whose divine creativity sparked the imagination of Tolkien and, by extension, the conception of this scholarly endeavor. In writing about the creation, providence, and eschatology nestled within the tales of Middle-Earth, it's impossible not to perceive the echoes of the Creator's song, reverberating through the ages and into our hearts.

This account of acknowledgment, though far from exhaustive, serves to express a deep-seated gratitude to all who have played a part in the realization of this work. May it stand as a testament to the enduring legacy of Tolkien's vision and the unsearchable riches of Roman Catholic theology.

In closing, let this endeavor inspire others to tread their paths of exploration, armed with the light of faith and the rich tapestry of Tolkien's mythopoeic universe. To all those who embark on such a quest, may you find both wisdom and wonder in equal measure.

References:

Chapter 15: Notes

In the preceding chapters, we have embarked on a comprehensive journey, tracing the harmonious and sometimes discordant melodies of Catholic doctrine through the mythopoeic tapestry woven by J.R.R. Tolkien. This chapter consolidates the numerous references, providing a structured compendium for further exploration and study.

Tolkien's creation narrative, as outlined in "The Silmarillion," echoes the intricate balance between divine providence and the exercise of free will. This equilibrium is foundational not only to Catholic theology but also to the moral and spiritual anatomy of Middle-Earth (Shippey, 2000). As such, the genesis of Eä and the unfolding Music of the Ainur serve as a prelude to the longstanding theological discourse on the coexistence of an omnipotent, benevolent Creator and the existence of evil, epitomized by the fall of Melkor.

Delving into the dual nature of Elves and Men, we encounter a poignant theological dialogue. The immortal Elves, with their yearning for the undying lands, and the mortal Men, entrusted with the gift of death, reflect the Catholic contemplation on the soul's longing for its true homeland with the Divine (Flieger, 2005). This juxtaposition illuminates the Catholic teachings on the nature of the soul, its immortality, and the existential journey towards achieving divine union.

The providential guidance witnessed through the eucatastrophic turns within "The Lord of the Rings" illustrate Tolkien's personal conviction in the ultimate triumph of good, a belief deeply rooted in his Catholic faith. The subtle yet profound interventions are reminiscent of the workings of grace in the world, guiding it towards an ordained end despite the apparent prevalence of darkness (Carpenter, 1977).

The eschatological themes present in "The Return of the King" are emblematic of the Catholic hope in the Second Coming of Christ. Through the restoration of the Kingdom of Gondor and the coronation of Aragorn, Tolkien articulates a vision of the world's renewal, a theme central to Christian eschatology.

Within the sacred realm of Middle-Earth, the sacramental imagination flourishes. Lembas bread and Miruvor, sustaining and reviving the travelers, symbolize the Eucharist, aligning with the Catholic understanding of sacramentals as means of divine grace (Caldecott, 2012). These elements, though fictional, invite reflection on the significance of sacraments in nourishing and fortifying the spiritual journey.

The Marian figures and virtues found in Middle-Earth, particularly the character of Galadriel, invite a contemplation on the role of the Virgin Mary within Catholic doctrine. Galadriel's narrative arc, embodying humility and service, parallels the veneration of Mary as the model of obedience and grace.

The theological discourse on freedom and predestination is vividly portrayed through the destinies interwoven in Middle-Earth's narrative fabric. The paradox of divine foreknowledge and free will finds its reflection in the characters' struggles, highlighting the Catholic teaching on God's omniscience and human agency.

The portrayal of death and the afterlife, explored through the diverging fates of Elves and Men, prompts a theological inquiry into the Catholic doctrines on mortality, immortality, and the soul's journey post-death. Tolkien's world, with its distinct eschatological vision, offers a creative reflection on these enduring questions.

The divine revelations through the Palantíri and the role of prophecy in Middle-Earth echo the Catholic understanding of divine revelation, tempered by the fallibility of human interpretation. This theme resonates with the challenges surrounding the interpretation of sacred scripture and the role of prophecy in guiding faith.

The beauty and sanctity of creation, celebrated throughout Tolkien's legendarium, serve as a reminder of the Catholic doctrine of creation ex nihilo and the Creator's omnipotence and benevolence. The reverence for nature, embodied by the Ents or the preservation ethos of the Elves, mirrors the Catholic call for stewardship of God's creation.

The linguistic dimension, particularly the Elvish languages, underscores the sanctity of the Word, aligning with the Catholic tradition that venerates the Logos. In Tolkien's philological creations, we glimpse a reflection of the divine, underscoring the inherent power and beauty of language.

The theological symbolism woven into the narrative of the Two Trees of Valinor and the creation and fate of the Silmarils encapsulate themes of sin, redemption, and divine mercy. These narratives, rich in Catholic symbolism, invite a deep theological reflection on the nature of evil, the necessity of atonement, and the boundless capacity for forgiveness.

The nuanced portrayal of women in Middle-Earth, through characters such as Eowyn, Galadriel, and others, offers a canvas for exploring the Catholic understanding of femininity, virtue, and the dignity of the individual. Tolkien's female characters, though fewer, demonstrate strength, wisdom, and grace, embodying the diversity of spiritual and moral virtues celebrated in Catholic teaching.

As we conclude this chapter, it is our hope that these notes serve as steady lanterns illuminating the path for those wishing to delve deeper into the confluence of Catholic doctrine and Tolkien's mythopoeia. In the vast expanses of Middle-Earth, as in the tapestry of Catholic theology, we find a rich dialogue between faith, reason, and imagination, inviting an ever-deeper exploration into the mysteries of the Divine and the human experience.

Chapter 16: Bibliography

As we draw to a close on our journey through the intersection of Catholic doctrine and Tolkien's mythopoetic universe, it is imperative to acknowledge the scholarly works that have illuminated our path. The bibliography presented here is not merely a list but a testament to the intricate dialogue between faith and fiction, theology and mythology, that has been the cornerstone of our exploration.

Our examination of creation, providence, and eschatology within Tolkien's narratives sought not just to defend but to elucidate the profound Catholic underpinnings of his work. To achieve this, we have leaned heavily upon a select compilation of academic resources that have themselves delved deep into the heart of Middle-Earth, uncovering the shimmering threads of divine truth woven into its fabric.

The works cited herein encompass a broad spectrum of perspectives, ranging from theological analysis to literary critique, each contributing to a fuller understanding of the material at hand. They serve as beacons, guiding us through the complex interplay of ideas that characterize Tolkien's creation and our interpretation thereof.

Among the sources, several have stood out for their insightful commentary on the symbiosis between Tolkien's fictional universe and the core tenets of Catholicism. These foundational texts have provided the bedrock upon which our discussions have been built, offering clarity and direction as we navigated the vast landscapes of Middle-Earth.

It is our hope that this bibliography will not only serve as a record of our intellectual journey but also as a resource for those who wish to embark on their own explorations. The journey into the depths of Tolkien's world is, much like the pilgrimage of faith, a never-ending quest for understanding and truth.

In light of this, the selection of works presented here is both an invitation and a challenge: an invitation to delve deeper into the mysteries of faith and fiction, and a challenge to view Tolkien's creations not merely as escapes from reality but as mirrors reflecting the divine.

As we conclude, let us remember that the conversation between theology and literature is ongoing, each continually enriching the other. May the resources listed below inspire further scholarship and contemplation, aiding in the defense and elucidation of Roman Catholic doctrine as seen through the prism of J.R.R. Tolkien's enduring legacy.

Without further ado, we present the bibliography that has undergirded our journey:

References

1. Aquinas, T. (n.d.). Summa Theologica. Christian Classics Ethereal Library.

2. Augustine, S. (397). Confessions. (E. B. Pusey, Trans.). Oxford: Oxford University Press.

3. Birzer, B. (2015). Tolkien's Sanctifying Myth: Understanding Middle-Earth. Wilmington: ISI Books.

4. Birzer, B. J. (2012). J.R.R. Tolkien's Sanctifying Myth: Understanding Middle-Earth. Wilmington, Del: ISI Books.

5. Caldecott, L. (2019). The Power of the Ring: The Spiritual Vision Behind the Lord of the Rings and The Hobbit. Crossroad. Caldecott's text delves into the Catholic symbolism embedded in Tolkien's mythology, offering compelling defenses of its doctrinal alignments.

6. Caldecott, S. (2012). The Power of the Ring: The Spiritual Vision Behind The Lord of the Rings. Crossroad.

7. Carpenter, H. (1977). J.R.R. Tolkien: A Biography. Houghton Mifflin.

8. Carpenter, H. (1977). J.R.R. Tolkien: A Biography. London: George Allen & Unwin.

9. Carpenter, H. (1977). The Letters of J.R.R. Tolkien. London: George Allen & Unwin.

10. Carpenter, H. (2019). J.R.R. Tolkien: A Biography. Houghton Mifflin Harcourt.

11. Carpenter, H. (Ed.). (1981). The Letters of J.R.R. Tolkien. Boston: Houghton Mifflin.

12. Catechism of the Catholic Church (CCC). (n.d.). Vatican.va. Retrieved from https://www.vatican.va/archive/ccc_css/archive/catechism/p1s2c1p4.htm

13. Catechism of the Catholic Church. (1993). Libreria Editrice Vaticana.

14. Catechism of the Catholic Church. (1994). 2nd Edition. Libreria Editrice Vaticana.

15. Catechism of the Catholic Church. (1997). 2nd ed. Vatican: Libreria Editrice Vaticana.

16. Catechism of the Catholic Church. (2000). 2nd ed. Vatican: Libreria Editrice Vaticana.

17. Flieger, V. (1997). A Question of Time: J.R.R. Tolkien's Road to Faërie. Kent, OH: Kent State University Press.

18. Flieger, V. (2002). A Question of Time: J.R.R. Tolkien's Road to Faërie. Kent State University Press.

19. Flieger, V. (2002). Splintered Light: Logos and Language in Tolkien's World. Grand Rapids: William B. Eerdmans Publishing Co.

20. Flieger, V. (2002). Splintered Light: Logos and Language in Tolkien's World. Kent State University Press.

21. Flieger, V. (2005). Interrupted Music: The Making of Tolkien's Mythology. Kent State University Press.

22. Flieger, V. (2005). Splintered Light: Logos and Language in Tolkien's World. Kent State University Press.

23. Genesis. (n.d.). In The Holy Bible (New International Version).

24. Gunton, C. E. (1998). The Triune Creator: A Historical and Systematic Study. Eerdmans.

25. Hammond, W.G., & Scull, C. (2005). The Lord of the Rings: A Reader's Companion. Houghton Mifflin Harcourt.

26. Holy Bible. Romans 8:28.

27. Isaiah 14:12-15. The Holy Bible.

28. John of the Cross, St. (n.d.). The Dark Night. Christian Classics Ethereal Library.

29. Lewis, C.S. (1964). The Discarded Image. Cambridge University Press.

30. New American Bible (Revised Edition). (n.d.). United States Conference of Catholic Bishops (USCCB). Retrieved from https://bible.usccb.org/bible

31. O'Neill, C. (2003). The Individuated Hobbit: Jung, Tolkien, and the Archetypes of Middle-Earth. Boston: Houghton Mifflin.

32. O'Neill, T. (2003). J.R.R. Tolkien: Myth, Morality, and Religion. HarperSanFrancisco.

33. Paul, S. (n.d.). Letter to the Romans 8:22. In The Holy Bible (New International Version).

34. Pearce, J. (2008). Tolkien: Man and Myth, a Literary Life. HarperCollins.

35. Pseudo-Dionysius. (n.d.). The Mystical Theology. Christian Classics Ethereal Library.

36. Shippey, T. (2000). J.R.R. Tolkien: Author of the Century. Houghton Mifflin.

37. Shippey, T. (2000). J.R.R. Tolkien: Author of the Century. London: HarperCollins.

38. Shippey, T. (2000). The Road to Middle-Earth: How J.R.R. Tolkien Created a New Mythology. Houghton Mifflin Harcourt.

39. Shippey, T. (2001). J.R.R. Tolkien: Author of the Century. HarperCollins.

40. Shippey, T. (2003). The Road to Middle-Earth. London: HarperCollins.

41. Shippey, T. (2005). The Road to Middle-Earth. London: HarperCollins.

42. Shippey, T.A. (2005). J.R.R. Tolkien: Author of the Century. HarperCollins.

43. The Holy Bible, New International Version. (2011). Biblica, Inc.

44. Tolkien, J.R.R. (1947). On Fairy-Stories. In Essays Presented to Charles Williams. Oxford: Oxford University Press.

45. Tolkien, J.R.R. (1954). The Fellowship of the Ring. United Kingdom: George Allen & Unwin.

46. Tolkien, J.R.R. (1954). The Lord of the Rings. London: George Allen & Unwin.

47. Tolkien, J.R.R. (1954). The Lord of the Rings. London: George Allen & Unwin.

48. Tolkien, J.R.R. (1955). The Return of the King. United Kingdom: George Allen & Unwin.

49. Tolkien, J.R.R. (1977). The Silmarillion. Houghton Mifflin.

50. Turner, A., & Turner, M. (2020). Finding God in The Hobbit. SaltRiver.

51. Wood, R. (2003). The Gospel According to Tolkien: Visions of the Kingdom in Middle-earth. Louisville, KY: Westminster John Knox Press.

52. Wood, R. (2018). Tolkien's Modern Reading: Middle-earth Beyond the Middle Ages. Cambridge University Press. This work provides an in-depth exploration of the various literary, philosophical, and theological influences on Tolkien's writing, shedding light on his integration of Catholic doctrine.

THE 15 PRAYERS OF ST. BRIDGET

These Prayers and these Promises have been copied from a book printed in Toulouse in 1740 and published by the P. Adrien Parvilliers of the Company of Jesus, Apostolic Missionary of the Holy Land, with approbation, permission and recommendation to distribute them.

Pope Pius IX took cognisance of these Prayers with the prologue; he approved them May 31, 1862, recognising them as true and for the good of souls.

As St. Bridget for a long time wanted to know the number of blows Our Lord received during His Passion, He one day appeared to her and said: "I received 5480 blows on My Body. If you wish to honour them in some way, say 15 Our Fathers and 15 Hail Marys with the following Prayers (which He taught her) for a whole year. When the year is up, you will have honoured each one of My Wounds."

He made the following promises to anyone who recited these Prayers for a whole year:

1. I will deliver 15 souls of his lineage from Purgatory.
2. 15 souls of his lineage will be confirmed and preserved in grace.
3. 15 sinners of his lineage will be converted.
4. Whoever recites these Prayers will attain the first degree of perfection.
5. 15 days before his death I will give him My Precious Body in order that he may escape eternal starvation; I will give him My Precious Blood to drink lest he thirst eternally.
6. 15 days before his death he will feel a deep contrition for all his sins and will have a perfect knowledge of them.

7. I will place before him the sign of My Victorious Cross for his help and defence against the attacks of his enemies.

8. Before his death I shall come with My Dearest Beloved Mother.

9. I shall graciously receive his soul, and will lead it into eternal joys.

10. And having led it there I shall give him a special draught from the fountain of My Deity, something I will not for those who have not recited My Prayers.

11. Let it be known that whoever may have been living in a state of mortal sin for 30 years, but who will recite devoutly, or have the intention to recite these Prayers, the Lord will forgive him all his sins.

12. I shall protect him from strong temptations.

13. I shall preserve and guard his 5 senses.

14. I shall preserve him from a sudden death.

15. His soul will be delivered from eternal death.

16. He will obtain all he asks for from God and the Blessed Virgin.

17. If he has lived all his life doing his own will and he is to die the next day, his life will be prolonged.

18. Every time one recites these Prayers he gains 100 days indulgence.

19. He is assured of being joined to the supreme Choir
    of Angels.

20. Whoever teaches these Prayers to another, will have
    continuous joy and merit which will endure eternally.

21. There where these Prayers are being said or will be
    said in the future God is present with His grace.

**Each prayer is preceded by one Our Father and one
Hail Mary.**

Our Father, who art in heaven, hallowed be thy name.
Thy kingdom come.
Thy will be done on earth as it is in heaven.
Give us this day our daily bread and forgive us our
trespasses as we forgive those who trespass against us and
lead us not into temptation but deliver us from evil. **Amen**

Hail Mary, full of grace, the Lord is with thee; blessed art
thou among women and blessed is the fruit of thy womb,
Jesus.
Holy Mary, Mother of God, pray for us sinners, now and at
the hour of our death. **Amen.**

FIRST PRAYER
Our Father – Hail Mary.

O Jesus Christ! Eternal Sweetness to those who love Thee, joy surpassing all joy and all desire, Salvation and Hope of all sinners, Who hast proved that Thou hast no greater desire than to be among men, even assuming human nature at the fullness of time for the love of men, recall all the sufferings Thou hast endured from the instant of Thy conception, and especially during Thy Passion, as it was decreed and ordained from all eternity in the Divine plan.

Remember, O Lord, that during the Last Supper with Thy disciples, having washed their feet, Thou gavest them Thy Most Precious Body and Blood, and while at the same time thou didst sweetly console them, Thou didst foretell them Thy coming Passion.
Remember the sadness and bitterness which Thou didst experience in Thy Soul as Thou Thyself bore witness saying: "My Soul is sorrowful even unto death."

Remember all the fear, anguish and pain that Thou didst suffer in Thy delicate Body before the torment of the Crucifixion, when, after having prayed three times, bathed in a sweat of blood, Thou wast betrayed by Judas, Thy disciple, arrested by the people of a nation Thou hadst chosen and elevated, accused by false witnesses, unjustly judged by three judges during the flower of Thy youth and during the solemn Paschal season.

Remember that Thou wast despoiled of Thy garments and clothed in those of derision; that Thy Face and Eyes were veiled, that Thou wast buffeted, crowned with thorns, a reed placed in Thy Hands, that Thou was crushed with blows and overwhelmed with affronts and outrages.
In memory of all these pains and sufferings which Thou didst endure before Thy Passion on the Cross, grant me before my death true contrition, a sincere and entire confession, worthy satisfaction and the remission of all my sins. **Amen.**

SECOND PRAYER
Our Father – Hail Mary.
O Jesus! True liberty of angels, Paradise of delights, remember the horror and sadness which Thou didst endure when Thy enemies, like furious lions, surrounded Thee, and by thousands of insults, spits, blows, lacerations and other unheard-of-cruelties, tormented Thee at will.

In consideration of these torments and insulting words, I beseech Thee, O my Saviour, to deliver me from all my enemies, visible and invisible, and to bring me, under Thy protection, to the perfection of eternal salvation. **Amen.**

THIRD PRAYER

Our Father - Hail Mary.

O Jesus! Creator of Heaven and earth Whom nothing can
encompass or limit, Thou Who dost enfold and hold all under
Thy Loving power, remember the very bitter pain.

Thou didst suffer when the Jews nailed Thy Sacred Hands
and Feet to the Cross by blow after blow with big blunt nails,
and not finding Thee in a pitiable enough state to satisfy
their rage, they enlarged Thy Wounds, and added pain to
pain, and with indescribable cruelty stretched Thy Body
on the Cross, pulled Thee from all sides, thus dislocating Thy
Limbs.

I beg of Thee, O Jesus, by the memory of this most Loving
suffering of the Cross, to grant me the grace to fear Thee
and to Love Thee. **Amen.**

FOURTH PRAYER

Our Father - Hail Mary.

O Jesus! Heavenly Physician, raised aloft on the Cross to
heal our wounds with Thine, remember the bruises which

Thou didst suffer and the weakness of all Thy Members which were distended to such a degree that never was there pain like unto Thine.

From the crown of Thy Head to the Soles of Thy Feet there was not one spot on Thy Body that was not in torment, and yet, forgetting all Thy sufferings, Thou didst not cease to pray to Thy Heavenly Father for Thy enemies, saying: "Father forgive them for they know not what they do."

Through this great Mercy, and in memory of this suffering, grant that the remembrance of Thy Most Bitter Passion may effect in us a perfect contrition and the remission of all our sins. **Amen**.

FIFTH PRAYER
Our Father – Hail Mary.
O Jesus! Mirror of eternal splendour, remember the sadness which Thou experienced, when contemplating in the light of Thy Divinity the predestination of those who would be saved by the merits of Thy Sacred Passion.

Thou didst see at the same time, the great multitude of reprobates who would be damned for their sins, and Thou didst complain bitterly of those hopeless lost and unfortunate sinners.

Through this abyss of compassion and pity, and especially through the goodness which Thou displayed to the good thief when Thou saidst to him: "This day, thou shalt be with Me in Paradise." I beg of Thee, O Sweet Jesus, that at the hour of my death, Thou wilt show me mercy. **Amen**.

SIXTH PRAYER
Our Father - Hail Mary.
O Jesus! Beloved and most desirable King, remember the grief Thou didst suffer, when naked and like a common criminal.

Thou was fastened and raised on the Cross, when all Thy relatives and friends abandoned Thee, except Thy Beloved Mother, who remained close to Thee during Thy agony and whom Thou didst entrust to Thy faithful disciple when Thou saidst to Mary: "Woman, behold thy son!" and to St. John: "Son, behold thy Mother!"

I beg of Thee O my Saviour, by the sword of sorrow which pierced the soul of Thy holy Mother, to have compassion on me in all my affliction and tribulations, both corporal and spiritual, and to assist me in all my trials, and especially at the hour of my death. **Amen**.

SEVENTH PRAYER

Our Father - Hail Mary.

O Jesus! Inexhaustible Fountain of compassion, Who by a profound gesture of Love, said from the Cross: "I thirst!" suffered from the thirst for the salvation of the human race.

I beg of Thee O my Saviour, to inflame in our hearts the desire to tend toward perfection in all our acts; and to extinguish in us the concupiscence of the flesh and the ardor of worldly desires. **Amen**.

EIGHTH PRAYER

Our Father - Hail Mary.

O Jesus! Sweetness of hearts, delight of the spirit, by the bitterness of the vinegar and gall which Thou didst taste on the Cross for Love of us, grant us the grace to receive worthily.

Thy Precious Body and Blood during our life and at the hour

of our death, that they may serve as a remedy and consolation for our souls. **Amen.**

NINTH PRAYER

Our Father – Hail Mary.

O Jesus! Royal virtue, joy of the mind, recall the pain Thou didst endure when, plunged in an ocean of bitterness at the approach of death, insulted, outraged by the Jews.

Thou didst cry out in a loud voice that Thou was abandoned by Thy Father, saying: "My God, My God, why hast Thou forsaken me?"

Through this anguish, I beg of Thee, O my Saviour, not to abandon me in the terrors and pains of my death. **Amen.**

TENTH PRAYER

Our Father – Hail Mary.

O Jesus! Who art the beginning and end of all things, life and virtue, remembers that for our sakes Thou was plunged in an abyss of suffering from the soles of Thy Feet to the crown of Thy Head.

In consideration of the enormity of Thy Wounds, teach me to keep, through pure love, Thy Commandments, whose way is wide and easy for those who love Thee. **Amen.**

ELEVENTH PRAYER

Our Father - Hail Mary.

O Jesus! Deep abyss of mercy, I beg of Thee, in memory of Thy Wounds which penetrated to the very marrow of Thy Bones and to the depth of Thy being, to draw me, a miserable sinner, overwhelmed by my offenses, away from sin and to hide me from Thy Face justly irritated against me, hide me in Thy wounds, until Thy anger and just indignation shall have passed away. **Amen.**

TWELFTH PRAYER

Our Father - Hail Mary.

O Jesus! Mirror of Truth, symbol of unity, bond of charity, remember the multitude of wounds with which Thou wast afflicted from head to foot, torn and reddened by the spilling of Thy adorable Blood. O great and universal pain, which Thou didst suffer in Thy virginal flesh for love of us! Sweetest Jesus! What is there that Thou couldst have done for us which Thou has not done!

May the fruit of Thy suffering be renewed in my soul by the faithful remembrance of Thy Passion, and may Thy love increase in my heart each day, until I see Thee in eternity: Thou Who art the treasure of every real good and every joy, which I beg Thee to grant me, O Sweetest Jesus, in heaven. **Amen.**

THIRTEENTH PRAYER
Our Father - Hail Mary.

O Jesus! Strong Lion, Immortal and Invincible King, remember the pain which Thou didst endure when all Thy strength, both moral and physical, was entirely exhausted, Thou didst bow Thy Head, saying: "It is consummated!"

Through this anguish and grief, I beg of Thee Lord Jesus, to have mercy on me at the hour of my death when my mind will be greatly troubled and my soul will be in anguish. **Amen.**

FOURTEENTH PRAYER
Our Father - Hail Mary.

O Jesus! Only Son of the Father, Splendour and Figure of His

Substance, remember the simple and humble
recommendation.

Thou didst make of Thy Soul to Thy Eternal Father, saying:
"Father, into Thy Hands I commend My Spirit!" And with Thy
Body all torn, and Thy Heart Broken, and the bowels of
Thy Mercy open to redeem us, Thou didst Expire.

By this Precious Death, I beg of Thee O King of Saints,
comfort me and help me to resist the devil, the flesh and the
world, so that being dead to the world I may live for Thee
alone.

I beg of Thee at the hour of my death to receive me, a
pilgrim and an exile returning to Thee. **Amen.**

FIFTEENTH PRAYER
Our Father – Hail Mary.
O Jesus! True and fruitful Vine! Remember the abundant
outpouring of Blood which Thou didst so generously shed
from Thy Sacred Body as juice from grapes in a wine press.

From Thy Side, pierced with a lance by a soldier, blood and
water issued forth until there was not left in Thy Body a

single drop, and finally, like a bundle of myrrh lifted to the top of the Cross Thy delicate Flesh was destroyed, the very Substance of Thy Body withered, and the Marrow of Thy Bones dried up.

Through this bitter Passion and through the outpouring of Thy Precious Blood, I beg of Thee, O Sweet Jesus, to receive my soul when I am in my death agony. **Amen.**

CONCLUSION

O Sweet Jesus! Pierce my heart so that my tears of penitence and love will be my bread day and night; may I be converted entirely to Thee, may my heart be Thy perpetual habitation, may my conversation be pleasing to Thee, and may the end of my life be so praiseworthy that I may merit Heaven and there with Thy saints, praise Thee forever. **Amen.**